UNLEARN DOGMA

Be Bold and Trail Blaze Your Path
to Wealth, Health and Wisdom

Zoë Cayetano

ISBN-13: 978-0-578-83727-7
ISBN-10: 0-578-83727-7

Library of Congress Control Number: 2018675309
Printed in the United States of America

This book is for informational purposes only. It should not
be considered Financial, Health or Legal Advice. Not all
information will be accurate. Consult a professional before
making any significant decisions.

https://unlearndogma.com

*For my mom, Aline, who has always seen my true
worth, and inspired me to reach for more and
create a world that I deserved.*

*For my partner in life, Jing, who has supported
me through my crazy ideas and for being my
accountability buddy to create the person I want to
become.*

*For my 15-year-old self who once thought that
publishing books is for a certain type of person, not
for herself; who held herself back and missed out
on amazing experiences that the world has to offer
because of old dogmas that didn't fit her story;
and, who forgone moments because of the many
self-limiting beliefs she held true and was careful
not to break.*

*For you who was forced to fit into a fabricated
mold; who was held back by old dogmas that didn't
fit your complex mind and intricate life experiences;
who feared the leap because it was out of the
ordinary; and, who wants to live a life that's full of
meaning, joy and surreal adventures.*

This book is for you.

CONTENTS

Title Page

Copyright

Dedication

Foreword

Why We Have Dogmas   1

Part 1: Dogmas of Wealth   4

Dogma #1: Money is Evil   9

Dogma #2: Wealth is Only for a Certain   14
Person

Dogma #3: It is Rude to Ask Someone How   21
Much She is Making

Dogma #4: Have a Secure and Well-paying   28
Job, and Then Work Every Day

Dogma #5: Your Net Worth is Based on Your   39
Salary

Dogma #6: Make Money from 9 a.m. to 5 p.m   45

Dogma #7: Save all of your money   49

Dogma #8: Money Makes the World Go   54

Round

Dogma #9: Have it All   59

Part 2: Dogmas of Health   63

Dogma #10: Trade Your Health for Success   67

Dogma #11: Leave It to the Professional   72

Dogma #12: Life is Short   78

Dogma #13: Just Take Medicine   83

Dogma #14: Focus on What's Wrong   88

Dogma #15: When I Become Successful, then   94
I'll be Happy

Dogma #16: Aging is Inevitable; Signs of   99
Aging are Normal

Part 3: Dogmas of Wisdom   102

Dogma #17: Be Good at One Thing and Stick   106
to It

Dogma #18: Follow Your Passion   114

Dogma #19: Your Degree IS Your Job Title   120

Dogma #20: Travel When You Retire   128

Dogma #21: It All Goes Downhill from Here   135

Dogma #22: Being Educated Means Having   141
a College Degree

Dogma #23: Stay Busy to be Productive   146

Dogma #24: Never Quit   152

Dogma #25: Listen to Experts   158

Afterword   163

About The Author   165

Praise For Author   167

Your Dogma Unlearning in Action   171

FOREWORD

Early to bed and early to rise, makes a man healthy, wealthy, and wise

— BENJAMIN FRANKLIN

During the time of writing this book, I was taking a week of vacation from a full-time job that I took right after college. As cliché as it may sound, I grew a lot this year—expanded what I knew, explored different ways of thinking, and created my own reality.

This book is inspired by many of the greats that I study, aiming to project their life's successes to mine. Since I was 16, I've looked up to the likes of Steve Jobs, Elon Musk and Richard Branson. It was

Steve Jobs who said it so brilliantly, "Life can be so much broader, once you discover one simple fact, and that is that everything you call 'life' was made up by people who were *no smarter than you.* And you can change it, you can influence it, you can build your own things that other people can use."

These words, and by now, my mantras, have truly changed the way I view the world. Starting at age 16, I started a fashion blog after just migrating with my family to the United States. I was then invited to cover Phoenix Fashion Week as media personnel and interviewed many prolific designers in the industry. At the same time, I worked an hourly job making pizzas and hosting birthday parties—just like any teenager my age. I quickly realized the value of money and working for luxuries I desired (at the time, it was a DSLR camera and a MacBook).

Rewinding much earlier than that, I didn't use to have a good handle on my finances. In fact, I had an unhealthy relationship with it. I was born in a religious household and growing up I was taught to view money as evil. It was money that destroyed relationships across my extended family and divorced my parents. It was money that made people greedy and selfish. It was money that swayed people to do evil.

So I thought...

Fast forward to now, I've come to the realization that money is just a tool—just like any other tool that enables you to do things and make things. It is money that enables you to build things that other people find value in. It enables you to see the world and experience life. It is money that can help you create your own reality.

I have always been ambitious and have been persevering to use my talents to change the world and create value for other people. In college, I pursued two degrees—in Applied Physics and Business Marketing. It was all in the hopes of bridging the two fields to create something of value for the world. I worked my ass off in college. At some point, I was taking six classes while working two jobs, one in a big tech firm and one as a researcher in a particle physics research lab.

Work and school came first. I would go to classes from 7 a.m., end work at 7 p.m. and return home to study until two in the morning—only to wake up at 5 a.m. to do it all over again. Taking on those two degrees and pursuing to excel at work also took away my weekends.

Everything else came second—my health, relationships, hobbies. I got sick a lot, and it took a long time for me to recover. It really took a toll on my wellbeing. I would take a pass on seeing my doctor, because between my crazy class and work schedules, I didn't really have any more time to dedicate to seeing my doctor (unless my doctor starts seeing patients at two in the morning, even then I would sacrifice my sleep that night).

At the time, I still didn't have a healthy relationship with my finances. Yeah, I would work overtime and get paid 1.5x for the hours I put in, but somehow still end up with not much money left in my bank account. At the surface, it looked like I was killing it. At 19, I was getting paid $32 per hour and $48 when I work overtime. It was also an internship at a big tech firm, so I pretty much secured a high-paying full-time job right out of college.

Graduation came and my bank account was still the same. I graduated from college at 21 with two degrees—and fortunately, because I went to a state university, with only $13,000 of student debt. This amount of student debt is manageable, believe it or not, knowing that the average student loan debt in the United States was $31,117 in 2019. The university I went to charged a base tuition rate of $7,500, excluding room and board, books, and other excessive fees for sporting events. Since I had a relatively high-paying internship by sophomore year, I was able to pay off my tuition in cash in the subsequent years. I was making $30,000-45,000 a year before taxes and had a living expense of about $750-1,000 a month.

It was only really after reading personal finance books and following the likes of Robert Kiyosaki and Warren Buffet that I finally got a better grip on my finances.

In Kiyosaki's book, "Rich Dad Poor Dad", he talks about the contrast of two lifestyles and relationships with money. On one hand, he had a father figure who was on the surface "rich", working for a corporate job, but under the hood, he was living paycheck-to-paycheck. On the other hand, he had another father figure who was on the surface "poor", owning a couple of small businesses, but under the hood, his money will outlive him and his family.

At the time, I was the former, at the surface, I was a 21-year-old, just coming out of college, earning six figures in a big tech firm, but still living paycheck-to-paycheck. I knew I had to make some changes and be on the latter boat.

This book is about creating your own reality in all matters of life, including money, health, and wisdom. I talk about the dogmas that I had to unlearn in order to achieve success and happiness in all of those matters.

I share the things I've learned along the way and viewpoints I've soon come to discover—all in the pursuit to build the life that brings me joy, allows me to cherish relationships that matter, and enable me to keep growing without sacrificing my health and wellbeing.

This was the self-help, motivational book I would have wanted to have. Many of the thoughts and ideas are compiled from many of my learnings from reading about many greats. I am standing on the shoulders of giants, and I am in no form claiming any of these ideas as my own. They were fitted to best fit my current situations and circumstances. What I have done is make the appropriate connections for my life, and that's what I'm hoping to share with you.

◆ ◆ ◆

The structure of this book

Having read many self-help books, I've come to realize that the books are only as useful as the actionable steps you can and choose to take. There are too many self-help books that are filled with cute, little motivational quotes but are lacking the gory details of what it really takes to go from where you are to where you want to be. In the hopes of making this book as useful as possible, I included specific and actionable steps that you can take. Look for them with the "One Thing You Can Do This Week" sections throughout the book.

Secondly, one other important note about how this book is structured is how I've divided the book into three sections: wealth, health, and wisdom. It goes without saying, you can apply the principles across all of these aspects. I may talk about a specific topic in the wealth section, but the lessons could apply to build wisdom. This is why this book is not a series of three books. I purposefully collected them into one book, so you can draw the appropriate connections and discover new ways of looking at things by applying what you know in one area to another.

Third, the first step in overcoming your self-limiting belief is to name it—identify what it is. This is an advice I've gotten from a public speaking coach who taught me how to present technical information to a technical audience. Often, a key objective of a technical presentation—whether you're presenting about your code or a new scientific finding—is to change the way the audience views a specific subject or issue. One powerful tactic in presenting with that objective in mind is to name the bias. In the beginning of your presentation, call out the bias or belief your audience might be holding that you aim to debunk or disprove. This allows your audience to pinpoint, then re-evaluate for themselves if what they believe in is wrong. In this book, I name the exact dogmas, go on to uncover why we may had been taught that dogma in the first place, and then show you the perils of blindly following this dogma and how they may be limiting you and your potential.

◆ ◆ ◆

What this book is not about

Throughout the book, I talk about specific examples of how I have done something. This book is not intended to show you the step-by-step tactics you need to implement in your life. This book is not about the specific tactics—our personal goals and scenarios may differ. For example, I talk about specific tactics I've implemented to gain wealth, but those tactics and scenarios could change one year or five years after publishing this book. This book is about the mindset shifts, dogmas I had to unlearn and the necessary philosophies I've learned in becoming wealthy, healthy, and wise, because I believe that all of these matters of life are a question of mindset. You need to ensure you understand these fundamentals before plunging into the specific activities that will get you there.

I intend for this book to be as evergreen as possible. This is also why I don't intend to direct you to specific websites in this book, because they may also change. I will consolidate helpful resources, where you can read more and use the same tools I use at **http://unlearndogma.com/BONUSES**.

◆ ◆ ◆

Just-in-time learning

I have personally taken a number of courses and read books, but what I found was it is most effective to learn something when you're in the middle of a crisis of some sort. When I built my own online store is when I learned the most about digital marketing. It wasn't when I took a digital marketing course in college.

I encourage you to skim the book for the first time. Familiarize yourself with the different components and topics of the book, and then jump to specific areas that interest you the most or are the most relevant to your specific situation right now. Pinpoint the specific dogmas you resonate with or fear that may be limiting you right now, then dive deeper into that section.

I'm excited to share all these lessons and the necessary mindset shifts I had to personally make in order to achieve the results I want in my life. I'm hoping you could take these principles for yourself and achieve a life that you enjoy with no compromises and no regrets.

❖ ❖ ❖

This book is for informational purposes only. It should not be considered Financial, Health or Legal

Advice. Not all information will be accurate. Consult a professional before making any significant decisions.

WHY WE HAVE DOGMAS

"When you grow up you tend to get told that the world is the way it is and your life is just to live your life inside the world. Try not to bash into the walls too much. Try to have a nice family life, have fun, save a little money. That's a very limited life. Life can be much broader once you discover one simple fact: Everything around you that you call life was made up by people that were no smarter than you. And you can change it, you can influence it... Once you learn that, you'll never be the same again."

— STEVE JOBS

Dogmas are beliefs that are passed on to generations. They are structures of thinking that allow us to process information and understand the world around us. After all, our senses send our brains roughly eleven million bits of information per second. This is expansively way more bits of information our conscious mind could ever process in a given second—our brains maxes out at an estimated fifty bits per second of processing.

It is our human ability to make and manipulate increasingly abstract mental representations (e.g., text from books, beliefs, traditions) that have allowed us to ascend in dominance in the food chain in a world of stronger, faster, sharper-toothed competitors.

It is our moral convictions and ideas that have allowed us to judge what is right or wrong. It was how the elderly passed on learned wisdom to future generations.

And in grasping these dogmas as truths we dismiss the myriad assumptions and circumstantial nature of these dogmas. We dismiss the fact that certain dogmas were made based on the specific point and time in history and the circumstances that prevailed then.

We ought to question and as necessary, unlearn these dogmas when they no longer apply. This is not to dismiss the generational wisdom that is passed on through these dogmas, but this is about critically thinking their merits. We shouldn't be accepting beliefs with a blind eye waiting for them to nip us in the butt when the time comes. This is about giving justice to what brought humanity to the top of the food chain in the first place—our ability to think, process and decide.

In turn, dogmas and our belief system are the fundamental basis of our actions. The dogmas we believe in shape our values, which in turn, shape our actions and our thoughts. These actions and thoughts, when repeatedly practiced, turn into habits. By altering what we fundamentally believe in, we could change the course of our lives. By unlearning dogmas that lead to self-limiting beliefs, we could expand the adjacent possible, and discover what's more to the world than what meets the eye. It is in this unlearning do we create breakthroughs. Physical, mental or emotional, breakthroughs allow us to see the other side of what used to be invisible to our eyes. The first step is to really evaluate the dogmas that have set forth the set of values we now follow, which in turn dictate how we choose and what actions we take.

Life is fluid and that very fluidity of life is what makes the human experience *so* human. It is in the ups and downs, and the twists and turns of our experiences that make life so interesting. Circumstances change, and dogmas should to. After all, part of what it means to be human is to adapt and evolve.

PART 1: DOGMAS OF WEALTH

G rowing up, I was taught the value and the perils of money at an early age. I saw how it broke families apart and encouraged vengefulness. In my household and in traditional Asian fashion, you are taught that success depends on getting a secure job that'll pay for day-to-day expenses and earn you money for retirement, which in turn, depends on getting a good education.

When my family moved to the United States, I knew I had to get to work right away. I was persistent that I was going to work for the American dream, which was to get a secure, 401(k)-matching job and own a house. Since age 16, I've put in hours for money. Day in, day out, I would work eight to ten hours and most oftentimes, during the weekends, too.

I bought into all of it—to the idea that there is no other way to be rich and successful but to work the hours and slave your life away to a stable job.

In the back of my mind, I knew that life had to be much, much broader than this. It had to be much bigger and more fruitful than working for forty years of your life in order to do the other things, like traveling, cherishing relationships, and experiencing life, only after you turn 59 and a half.

I knew that there has to be more to life than this...

I studied the greats, read books, watched self-made billionaires, and pursued to understand the secrets to their success. This portion of the book is all about the necessary mindset shifts that I needed to make and dogmas I had to unlearn in order to have a healthier relationship with money. Throughout, I included practical advice and the next steps that you can follow to achieve financial freedom for yourself.

To make peace with money as a tool as opposed to the fruit of all evil, I had to make the realization that money is a tool. It's a tool that not only can buy you a yacht but can also build schools, fund cancer research and provide value to society.

I also had to make the realization that it is accessible to everyone. You can make it happen for yourself.

In fact, most billionaires in the world are self-made. Most billionaires didn't get rich by inheriting trust funds or outsized family businesses. Most billionaires were normal civilians like you and I. The difference between them and us is that they have a healthy relationship with money. They've understood how to harness what they know to build off wealth that will outlive them.

Once I figured out the financial dogmas that became the limiting beliefs that held me back from achieving financial freedom, I was able to build multiple sources of income, become debt-free, opened a retirement account, and most importantly, have a much better emotional reaction and mental state when it comes to matters of money.

dogma #1

"Money is Evil"

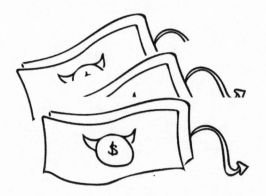

DOGMA #1:
MONEY IS EVIL

"Money is not evil by itself; it's just paper with perceived value to obtain other things we value in other ways."

– MORGAN FREEMAN

G rowing up in a religious household and attending Catholic school from primary to secondary school, I was taught "The love of money is a root of all kinds of evil," which was a reference to Timothy 6:10 from the Bible.

In my household, we never talked about money. We avoided the topic like it was the plague. And if we ever did, the conversations were deeply rooted in pride, vengeance, and hurtful words.

The Philippines is a melting pot of a diverse and rich history rooted in Asian and Spaniard culture. What you get is an interesting combination of a culture that values hard work, patience, communal ties, and family name pride.

It was common for a tricycle driver to ask you what your last name was. If someone doesn't know you, personally, he sizes you up based on what he knows about your family ties. He then draws up conclusions about who you are, where you live and the latest gossip about a family member.

As primates, we use heuristics to reduce the mental effort required to make decisions. In this case, the driver was just trying to be efficient at knowing who I am, and of course, where I live, so he could drive me there as I was commuting.

This culture of hard work and family name pride results in a double-edged sword. On the one end, growing up with such high expectations pushes you to move up and move really fast. On the other, you live life avoiding any situations you may find yourself in that puts your family name to shame.

The rich get richer, they say.

They get richer thanks to the law of compounding effects and generational wealth transfers. Especially in my hometown, land titles can be doctored, and all that's left for you to reclaim your so-called earned wealth is your family name. Land ownership was such a controversial topic at family dinners, whether it's some other relative trying to claim rights to a property or another relative asking for a handout.

Ever since I was young, it's been instilled in me, time and time again, dinner after dinner, that money is evil and that it is the root of all evil. And I've lost sight of the fact that money can be the root of evil and it can also be the root of love.

You just have to not lose sight of that.

I've studied too many of the greats that had used money for good. They have used money to build new companies, help look for a cure for diseases, and create value for other people.

Early on, I've discovered that I care very deeply about making an impact, and I aim to leave a positive impact on this world.

Money is just simply a tool that exaggerates *who you are*. If you were already greedy and selfish, you're just going to get even more greedy and selfish with more wealth. On the flip side, if you are already generous and kind, you're just going to get even more generous and kind with it. It is simply a tool that lets you do more—whatever that more is.

The moment I stopped thinking of money as

evil was the moment I started really learning about money how it works. I realized that if you never learn how money works, you will never make money work for you.

dogma #2

"Wealth is only for a certain person"

DOGMA #2: WEALTH IS ONLY FOR A CERTAIN PERSON

"The key to abundance is meeting limited circumstances with unlimited thoughts."

– MARIANNE WILLIAMSON

"**G**ood for them, not for me," I told myself as I watch self-made billionaires make riches out of riches and become even wealthier.

For too long, I've played the victim and focused on my setbacks as opposed to creating the unborn opportunities that I can make for myself. I've focused on the fact that I was born in a third world country with a family that lives from paycheck to paycheck. I've rehearsed, many times in my head, that mantra that people like me (a woman from a minority background) get paid less in this world.

For far too long, I've been held back by my self-doubts and have *thought myself poor*. Seeing money as evil or the root of it, I've ignored my balance sheets. I avoided quantifying what I was making and spending. I avoided thinking and dreaming of riches.

I've made myself believe that wealth was distributed way before my time, and I can't do anything about it. There is no abundance in the world. When in fact, a majority of the wealthy today are self-made. The pie is not stagnant and it doesn't stop growing or reducing in size. You just have to create more value in the world that would then increase the shape of the pie. You are in control of the size of the pie. Self-made rich people have had to create something that society finds valuable in order to increase the size of the pie and create wealth for themselves.

I've had to shift my mindset. I've had to believe that I can make riches for myself. I've had to believe that I can get paid more than my male counterparts or those from a different ethnic background. I've had to disown the title of a poor person and the mental beliefs that this kind of life is for other people, not for me.

Once you make that mindset shift, you soon realize that it is not that complicated to get there.

At 22, I've set a goal for myself that by the age of 25, I will make six figures a month, not a year. From there, I've come to understand the necessary steps to get there and break the steps down into the fundamentals.

One of the keys to success in many greats is *desire.* If you can pinpoint what you want, you're going to more likely achieve it. You can't just leave it up to chance or luck. Doors don't wait for you to open them. You got to learn to build your doors, windows, and heck, the entire house.

To achieve what I want, I had to understand what I can achieve and remove any limiting be- liefs I had for anything short of what I can now believe I can achieve. Having these goals in mind helped me create definite steps in achieving great riches. It turned my dreams into a real milestone. I needed to become money conscious until the desire for great riches encouraged me to create a definite plan to get there.

In order to get there, I've had to realize that money is just a tool that exaggerates who you already are and that wealth is abundant. The size of the wealth pie can get bigger the more value to society you could create.

The reality is that everyone has the same opportunity to be rich. Some may face greater challenges than others, but the opportunity is there for everyone to seize.

One Thing You Can Do This Week

Auditing your assets and your liabilities

First, understand your assets. What are your sources of income? A good way to classify them is by understanding these seven sources of income that most millionaires have:

Earned Income. This is the money that you earn working for someone in a job, whether it's an hourly or salary pay.

Profit Income. This is the money that you make by selling something that costs you less to make or produce.

Interest Income. This is the money you gain from lending money to someone else, like putting it in a savings account, lending it to the government in the form of bonds, etc.

Dividend Income. This is the money you earn as a result of owning shares of a company.

Rental Income. This is the money you earn as a result of owning an asset and renting it out, like a property or a building.
Capital Gains. This is the money you get as a result of an increase in the value of your assets (s), like a company share or a house.

Royalty Income. This is the money you get by allowing someone else to use your ideas, processes, and products, like a photo you share on Shutterstock or a song you write.

Once you identify your assets, you need to identify your liabilities. Examples of which are student loan debts, home mortgages, credit card debts, and living expenses.

From here, you can identify the ratio of your expenses compared to your income, and your first goal will first be to decrease your liabilities and increase your assets.

Your goals will probably look different from mine. You can start pinpointing your financial goals by first looking at your necessary living expenses (e.g., food, shelter, electricity) and then identifying the other expenses you had forgone and set aside for after retirement (e.g., traveling, giving back). From these expenses, you can pinpoint the necessary income to expense ratio you will need to live comfortably and the way you want. Now, you have to find ways to expand your assets. You need to diversify and expand assets that are not dependent on you putting time into it in order to grow. A more sustainable path is to create asset types that could grow without you putting 9-5 hours into it every weekday, and can still work for you even when you're sick, you're on vacation or you're sleeping.

This is the reason why the idea of creating passive income has been so romanticized. What's not to love? You make money work for you while you're sleeping or on a backpacking expedition to Bali. We no longer have to depend on earned income, which is working a job where you have to trade your time for that income.

dogma #3

"It is rude to ask someone how
much she is making"

DOGMA #3:
IT IS RUDE TO
ASK SOMEONE
HOW MUCH SHE
IS MAKING

"You can't manage what you can't measure"

– PETER DRUCKER

I used to dread looking at bank statements, student loan dashboards, and expense receipts. I had attached many negative emotions to money. I avoided quantifying anything that has to do with money. When the topic of money gets brought up in conversations, my stress levels suddenly increase and my anxiety kicks in. I was so emotional when it came to all matters of money, so I avoided looking at it, analyzing and quantifying anything.

This behavior was learned. I remember during my internship, as naive as I was with the standards and taboos in America, I asked one of my co-workers how much he was getting paid. Little did I know, it's one of the taboo topics of conversations along with religion and politics, especially in the workplace. You don't ask other people what they make. My co-worker then went on to lecture me about not asking that question but also proceeded to tell me his salary range anyway, just because he was also one of my mentors. He told me that it was rude to ask how much someone makes. How would I know that it was? I was new to the country and new to the workforce.

But I should've known. My parents did teach me better than that. When I was younger, the elders in our household would never let the kids hear conversations about money. It never gets talked about at the dining table. Although, a little nosey me would always want to sneak and listen in to those conversations. The conversations were almost always about how a relative of ours is causing some drama because of some inherited property title.

Property titles were always very messy back in the Philippines. It was mostly due to the lack of standards, lack of proper information infrastructure, and bribery. You could always get a document under your name or falsify information if you had the right connections and the right amount of money. Needless to say, I was never taught how to handle money or how to have healthy conversations about it. I started to develop an emotional attachment to all matters of money. I developed negative emotions around it. It was money that encouraged many of my relatives to develop a strong distaste for each other. It was money that would split my family members apart. It was money that caused many familial fights and misunderstanding, and our nightly dose of someone yelling at someone in the house.

The necessary mindset shift I had to make is that it is not rude to ask someone how much they're making. It is rude to judge someone based on how much they're making. We need to talk about money more often, but it has to not be deeply rooted in hate, judgment, greed, and fear. We should be able to talk about money just like any other tool, like a hammer. It's never been tabooed to talk about a hammer.

I knew I needed to be money conscious in order to achieve my financial goals. I needed to be able to have a healthy and objective conversation with others about money.

One Thing You Can Do This Week
Find an accountability buddy

Find an accountability buddy whom you can share your financial goals with and encourage each other to reach those goals.
I'm very lucky to have found someone who shares a lot of the same characteristics as me. For me, it was my best friend who's also my partner in life.

We're both immigrants who came from poor families but had a lot of fire in us and desire to achieve greater and bigger things for ourselves. He supported me with all of the projects I would start and encouraged me to keep going. We became really comfortable talking about money to each other. He was actually the one who instilled in me the value of money as a tool—in that, you need money to actually do good in the world.

In the beginning, it was very difficult. I have never been one to share with anyone the behind-the-scenes of what I was hoping to accomplish and where I wanted to go. I've been so used to only letting people in when I had something to show for it. I would only tell anyone about anything once I accomplished what I set out to accomplish. In my mind, I was thinking I was somehow going to jinx it. In the end, I figured it was because I was scared of not being perfect. I was scared that how someone viewed me would change if I under-delivered on what I said I was going to do.

Then I realized, "Wait, I actually need that!" No matter what—we are social creatures. We seek acceptance from our tribe. That's how we prevailed. I needed someone who would actually give me a hard time if I didn't do what I said I was going to do. That's the whole point of having an accountability buddy in the first place. It took quite some time for me to actually build the muscle of learning to accept criticism and actually get to the point of being so obsessed with personal growth and self-development that whenever you hear criticism, you see opportunity. An accountability buddy would give you that kind of perspective that will only help you be better.

Our conversations about money became less of a mentally draining and emotional topic. The conversations became more like problems-solving tasks. We were both trained in a STEM field. I studied Physics in college, and he studied Computer Science. We were both trained as problem solvers. We were looking at our finances and financial goals as if they were math problems to solve. We were able to disentangle emotions from the viewpoint and adopt a stoic way of analyzing our personal finances.

Because we both became adamant about quantifying our finances, we were able to pinpoint the reasons why each month was an up or down month. We were able to focus resources and correct mistakes because we had understood where the money was flowing in and out of.

In the meantime, if you haven't found an accountability buddy yet, you could start journaling. Check in on your goals and archive your thoughts through a journal. Be your own accountability buddy, but actually jot things down and schedule them into time-based milestones, so you could come back to your notes and assess.

dogma #4

"Have a Secure and Well-paying Job, and Then Work Every Day"

DOGMA #4:
HAVE A SECURE AND WELL-PAYING JOB, AND THEN WORK EVERY DAY

"If you don't have any residual or passive income, or at least a plan on a residual income, you're living a very risky life. There is no security in a job, even in a high paying one. Be smart and don't rely on just one source of income."

– RAY HIGDON

Now, I'm not going to try to encourage you to quit your job and start a YouTube channel and make tons of money from affiliate marketing. That's for another book. What I do want to share with you is this necessary mindset shift that you don't have to depend on one income source.

If you're anyone like me, you were taught to land that one perfect job that will take care of my expenses until you retire. My first job right out of college was with a big tech firm. I saw this mindset across many of my colleagues. Many of them had been working there for 20+ years but were still in this rat race of living from paycheck to paycheck until they're 59. Many had a multiple six-figure a year salary but only a fraction afforded even a week of vacation. Many were tied to their desks from 9 a.m. to 5 p.m.—only taking their first vacation after eight years (even then, not every 9-5 job offers sabbatical leaves to employees).

Besides, what many rich people know is that paying income tax will keep you broke. This amount of income tax compounds the more money you make from an employer. The higher in the income bracket you fall on, the more you pay on income tax if you work for a corporation.

My story goes back to when I was in fourth grade. I've always been what you could call a hustler. Back in the Philippines, we have a market called Divisoria, where you could buy goods in bulk for very cheap—kind of like a physical and an older version of dropshipping. Whenever my mom would take us to the city, I would come with her to Divisoria and buy bulk goods from my savings. The goods ranged from toys to pencil cases, to LEGO blocks. I would then sell them at school. I earned my first Profit Income.

I saw my second, non-traditional source of income when I started blogging at age 16. I was making money from ads on my blog and a YouTube channel. Now, it wasn't a lot of money, but it allowed me to think creatively of other ways of gaining wealth.

From there, I started to earn money by writing on Medium. Then, I opened my online store, where I would source products from a Chinese manufacturer and dropship through Shopify.

At the same time, I started to invest in stocks through Robinhood and the Employee Stock Share Plan that the big tech firm offered. I started to generate income through Profit, Dividends, Royalties, and Interests on top of my Earned Income from the big tech firm.

It is indeed true that "A rising tide raises all

ships." Once I started to see the seeds would bear fruit, I soon realized other opportunities to even more money. This is the secret that has made many billionaires even richer. They knew that once you accumulate money from one source of income (e.g. Earned Income), you can then re-invest that money back to another source of income (e.g. Dividend Income from stocks) and make even more money. Make your money work for you, not the other way around.

What I also realized is that I don't have to trade my time for money. It was when I made these new sources of income that I realized that I don't have to put in every waking hour of my youth to generate income. The first Medium post I wrote still generates passive income for me every day, and I no longer have to put in any more of my time to generate money from it. I have also built up my stock portfolio with dividends paying stocks that pay a lump sum every month or every quarter depending on which stock or fund it was.

Now, I am in no way encouraging anyone to copy the same tactics I am using to generate new income sources. I am only sharing these to show you what is possible because only after reading about or watching others who have generated these sources of income for themselves is when I started to realize what is possible for me. In another portion of this book on Wisdom, I talk about passions and how to create opportunities that lend to great riches for yourself.

I understood that you don't necessarily have to trade your time for money. You can either input time or money, which will then generate you a source of income after the work is all done. What billionaires also knew is that their time is more valuable than money. After studying many self-made billionaires, from investors to celebrities, I've realized that a bigger portion of their income comes from sources where they don't have to trade their time for money (i.e. Earned Income). For most of them, they no longer have to put in eight or even ten hours of each day to get a paycheck. Their riches now come from other sources, like Dividends, Capital Gains, and Royalties. For most, they started with an Earned Income source, which then allowed them to invest in stocks or create a personal brand that in turn now pays them Dividends or Royalties Income.

Throughout my brief life and books I've read, I've learned that the rich has one thing in common: *none of them are employed.*

In school, I was taught that what will get you ahead is hard work and a stable, high-paying career. The idea of a constant stream of income that comes every fifteen days was romanticized as the stability that we should be desiring for ourselves. The very aspiration of stability that had been engrained to us of what success looks like is the very dogma that keeps us from progressing.

The reason why the rich gets richer is that they hardly take their financial situations for granted. They are risk takers, but calculated risk takers at that. They are always on the lookout for unfavorable changes. They dedicate time and effort to care for their riches and mitigate against unfavorable events.

After all, putting your eggs into one basket, just like only depending on a salary to keep up with your expenses and any unfavorable changes that could occur in your life is what is risky and not at all stable.

As much as we'd like to put an emphasis on the key to success is hard work, that is not necessarily how it works when you're employed. At 23, I became a people manager at a big tech company. I learned that by the time a new cycle of performance reviews and rewards come, the human resources department roll out their well-thought out strategy for employee retention and risk mitigation. The strategy consisted of looking at the overall employee population across the world, since the company operated worldwide. They took into account the macroeconomic, political and environmental factors in the world.

This is the reality of bonuses and the increase of your salary when you are employed. Your actual

performance and how hard you've worked are the
last factors they look into after all of the macro
factors that they need to mitigate against and account for to keep the company going and thriving.

This is why you should unlearn the dogma that
stability comes from one type of income source
(i.e., earned income from being employed), and instead look to diversify.

◆ ◆ ◆

One Thing You Can
Do This Week
Act and act fast

Have you ever had an idea that popped in your
mind in the middle of taking a shower? A lot of
us have. I go back to Les Brown saying that "The
graveyard is the richest place on earth because it
is here that you will find all the hopes and dreams
that were never fulfilled, the books that were
never written, the songs that were never sung, the
inventions that were never shared, the cures that
were never discovered, all because someone was
too afraid to take that first step, keep with the
problem, or determined to carry out their dream."

Many entrepreneurs and startup investors talk
about the idea of failing fast to succeed sooner.

Now, think about how you can implement that into your life. What I'd like for you to do is to adopt the habit of implementing fast.

Have any unborn opportunities stuck in your mind? Spend some time thinking of ways in how you can create something now. It was Peter Thiel that once said, "If you have a 10-year plan of how to get [somewhere], you should ask: 'Why can't you do this in 6 months?'"

Confidence grows by doing. You learn the most by actually getting out there and learning.

I've read many self-development books and even go to extreme lengths like taking classes in college that were not required just to simply learn. I took a class on Digital Marketing in college, but it was only really when I had started my store selling and marketing online did I learn what it truly took to market digitally. You get to learn all of the nuances and experience the many ups and downs in a project or a business by actually doing it. By actually going through all of the ups and downs yourself you will not only learn the tricks of the trade but also understand what works and what doesn't.

Skills stick better if you have a memory you can look back to to a time when something didn't work and you had to spend hours and hours to figure out how to make it work.

I even go to the extent of journaling the things that I put off doing and things that scare me the most. When I was young, my mom would take me and my brother to these resorts with high, winding slides to the pools. I had a love-hate relationship with those scary slides. On one hand, I knew I enjoyed the exhilaration of going through the slides. On the other hand, the slides looked so scary. I would often bitch out when it's almost my turn to go through the slides, but when it's over, I realized how much fun I have going through them. The fun and joy I get from going through those slides became much greater than my fears at the moment.

And this kept happening over and over again. I'm an ambivert. I'm flaky when it comes to going out and hanging out with friends. Before going out, my head turns to all of the excuses of why I shouldn't go out and hang out with my friends —my introversion kicks in. I always want to just cancel and come up with an excuse not to go. But then, when I do go, things always turn out much better. I have so much fun and always think to myself, "Why don't I do this more often?" Then I remember that whatever it is, whether it's fear, anxiety, or just plain laziness, gets in the way of me doing the things I want and enjoy doing.

What I encourage you to do is to just take the plunge. Act fast. Act so fast that your mind doesn't get to think of any more excuses not to do something. You will surprise yourself and discover many things that give you joy.

dogma #5

"Your Net Worth is Based on
Your Salary"

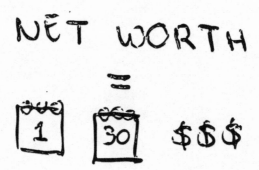

DOGMA #5: YOUR NET WORTH IS BASED ON YOUR SALARY

"Focus on all four of your net worth factors: increasing your income, increasing your savings, increasing your investment returns, and decreasing your cost of living by simplifying your lifestyle."

– T. HARV EKER

One other peril of asking someone how much they're making is your judgment may not be accurate. What someone is making from an Earned Income job may not be the complete picture. She may also own a real estate property that provides her income through Capital Gains, so if you're going to judge someone by how much they're making, then think twice.

Another mindset shift I had to make is to focus on increasing my assets.

I mentioned that your first goal needs to be decreasing your liabilities and increasing your assets.

When I was shamed for asking my co-worker how much money they're making, what I also didn't realize is that your net worth is not based on your monthly salary (well, it's not just based on your monthly salary). This is how you escape the rat race of living from one paycheck to another, month on month.

I made the realization that I need to make money work for me, as opposed to me working for money. I needed to build assets that will pay dividends even when I sleep. This is also the complete shift of not trading time for money.

I built an online store selling posture correcting bands, and because it was online, I wasn't tethered to any one physical location or time zone. I was printing money as I slept. I was able to sell to buyers on the other side of the world. I've inputted time and effort upfront and one to two hours during my daytime to make money throughout the day and at night. This is the beauty of a globalized economy. I was sitting in my California apartment while my buyer was in Singapore. Making my first sale while I was sleeping and getting money as soon as I opened my eyes were exhilarating and empowering. I had just proven to myself that it is possible and that I don't have to trade my time for money. I don't have to waste all of my time during the day working at a desk and not experiencing life, seeing the beauty of the world, and doing more with my life.

This experience snowballed into new opportunities. Because I learned new skills and tools in digital marketing through opening my first online store, I was able to uncover new opportunities that I could create for myself that could transfer the learnings across a completely different area. I started to build new assets.

I focused every free time I had in building new assets and re-invested my Earned Income to assets that will pay Dividends and Interest. This was the secret of the rich. This is how the rich keep getting richer, and you can too. What's more, multiple streams of income build stability and de-risks you for potential downfalls from one income stream (e.g. job layoffs).

When you quantify your net worth, you need to quantify the complete picture. On top of your Earned Income, you need to add the other sources of income and track it. Think of ways to add on to your list of assets and note what type of asset it is.

One Thing You Can
Do This Week
Your skill-asset-income matrix

Audit your skills and areas that interest you. On another column, brainstorm at least one way you can build an asset off of that skill or interest.

Here's an example

Skill: Digital marketing

Asset (Income): Online store (Profit income); Publish and market ghost-written books (Royalty income); Digital marketing and platform stocks e.g., Shopify (Interest and dividends income)

Here's an example table you can use for yourself:
Skill:

Asset (Income): e.g. Digital marketing
e.g. Online store
e.g. Profit income

Practice this often and you will soon develop a muscle of creating new opportunities and finding new ways to build assets.

dogma #6

"Make money from
9 a.m. to 5 p.m."

DOGMA #6: MAKE MONEY FROM 9 A.M. TO 5 P.M

"Don't waste your life living someone else's dream. Don't try to to emulate the people who came before you to the exclusion of everything else, contorting into a shape that doesn't fit."

– TIM COOK

I n my job in a big tech firm, my calendars are usually booked with meetings throughout the day. Oftentimes, I've had to start work at 6 a.m., so that I could get some real work done. I felt that I was always trying to catch up. I was being operated by my calendar, and my inbox became an ever-growing list of to-dos that anyone in the world could pile tasks on. I knew I had to change things and get rid of the old dogma of making money from 9 a.m. to 5 p.m.

We've been so trained to think that we need to be working during the hours of 9 a.m. to 5 p.m. The Bureau of Labor Statistics confirmed that the average American works 8.8 hours every day. It was in the late 18th century when companies, especially those operating in manufacturing facilities, started to implement eight-hour workdays in order to maximize operations uptime and profit margins. This standard was adopted by many companies – creating highly efficient and cost-effective factory workers.

What's more, an average American starts in the workforce at age 16 and works an hourly job, where we are trained to believe that working long is important and valued by employers. I worked an hourly job when I was 16 and being my over-achieving self, I was the type of hourly worker that would cover shifts from others and make overtime hours in order to maximize my return. In college, this training was even more strongly perpetuated with an internship that pays hourly. I was getting paid for working eight hours a day for five days a week is the standard, and that working long hours maximizes my pay.

However, the human brain can only focus for a

much shorter window of time than that. There's an inverse compounding effect to our productivity when we keep pushing the spreads of time we work with no breaks.

Coming out of college, I've read "The 4-Hour Workweek" by Tim Ferris, where he talks about generating income on auto-pilot and creating systems that automate your work, so you can essentially work four-hour weeks. Only then did I revisit this old dogma of stretching the duration to which I get certain work done in order to maximize my return.

What rich people know too well is the most valuable asset they could ever own is their time. They can't trade or buy more of it, so we need to spend our time wisely. Every hour you save, the more time you have to invest in yourself—learn something new, expand your network and spend your time however you want.

dogma #7

"Live frugally"

DOGMA #7:
SAVE ALL OF
YOUR MONEY

"Set your mind on a definite goal and observe how quickly the world stands aside to let you pass."

– NAPOLEON HILL

"**W**e can't afford that," I would constantly hear every time I would show up with a new piece of toy going shopping with my mom.

If you come from a poor family, you are most likely familiar with living frugally and the principle of living below your means. I have had my fair share of putting something in my grocery cart only to put it back when your totals exceed a certain amount. I was always taught to be very frugal and re-look at every expense with a keen eye.

What I had to learn is instead of saying to myself, "I can't afford that," I needed to challenge myself and instead ask *"How* can I afford that?"

When, in fact, the phrase "I can't afford that" quickly shuts off our problem-solving minds. It rids us of having to think of solutions to make more money in order to afford something. Secondly, what's instilled in that is also the thinking "We're poor. Save money." This statement is not a growth mindset. It assumes that you are never going to progress in life.

This was something I've had to re-look at, especially for high-quality grocery items. In the past, I would just buy the cheapest and quickest (i.e., microwavable) lunch I could get from the store. This was even with my aspirations of becoming a centenarian. I've always preached about taking care of your health, but when it came down to trading off money versus good food, I chose money. This, especially, didn't help when I was in hustle mode, always working. I wasn't focusing on what was important. Being poor leads to a poor diet, which eventually leads to diseases and disorders and even more medical expenses.

Now I have turned things around. I prioritize giving my body the fuel it needs (and good quality fuel, too). Now instead of saying "I can't afford that" to my organic produce aisle, I say "How can I afford that?" This gets me into problem-solving mode—into living the kind of lifestyle I want.

Today, I splurge on investments on my health and wellbeing, high quality of life, and assets that could work for me, such as dividends-paying stocks or REITs.

This is not to say that you shouldn't live frugally at all. I think in fact, you need to live frugally. Remember, we are trying to increase our assets and decrease our liabilities. You just have to look at what you're spending on more holistically.

Take, for example, buying organic, high quality food vs buying a new Chanel purse. One is an investment on yourself and is going to help you live a better and healthier life, while the other depreciates in value.

Investments in your health, personal growth and learning appreciate in value, while investments in physical goods depreciate.

Now, you should take these specific examples with a grain of salt, because value for you may mean different things. Perhaps investing in a Chanel purse or a yacht that at the surface depreciates in value could mean greater happiness.

You have to assess this distinction for yourself, and what you value and what brings you happiness. For me, my guilty pleasure is traveling and investing in creating memories. For others, that is a waste of money. Traveling and seeing that world with my own eyes are what's important to me right now, and that's what I've decided for myself.

dogma #8

"Money makes the world go round"

DOGMA #8: MONEY MAKES THE WORLD GO ROUND

"What if changing the world was just about being here, by showing up no matter how many times we get told we don't belong, by staying true even when we're shamed into being false, by believing in ourselves even when we're told we're too different? And if we all held on to that, if we refuse to budge and fall in line, if we stood our ground for long enough, just maybe... The world can't help but change around us."

– ELLIOT FROM MR. ROBOT TV SHOW

Money is a social construct and it depends on people agreeing upon what is less and more valuable in the world. Money doesn't make the world go round. It is the social agreements and constructs that make the world go round. People have to find high value in what you're selling for them to pay a premium for it.

We are a social species that depend on other people to move up in the world.

If you've ever taken an Economics class, you know that money is three things: storage of value, unit of account, and medium of exchange.

Money relies on our perceived value of something, accountability, and interaction or exchange between two parties. Those are all social acts.

Even if you're not a salesman that depends on someone buying something of value from you, you may be an engineer that depends on your ability to sell yourself to management to move up the ranks or become a principle engineer.

Having received formal training in the sciences, maths, and engineering, I know that these so-called "soft skills" are avoided like the plague. It is looked down upon and treated as if they were of lower value. When in fact, these soft skills are what enable us to make the world go round because the world goes round because of social agreements and constructs.

Your technical prowess may be the thing that gets you through the door, but your soft skills are the ones that will allow you to stay in the room.

Let's not romanticize soft skills being of lower value, and instead see soft skills are skills that are hard to automate. It is what will distinguish us from the cohort of like-minded individuals who have mastered the same amount of programming languages.

You could ask any day trader or any poker player that winning depends on learning, predicting and leveraging human psychology. Venture capitalists invest in the people behind a new firm — the business it makes them is the aftermath of investing into the people. Professions that depend largely on instincts, like law and finance, rely on someone's ability to predict someone else's next move and how they would react to a certain circumstance.

Money doesn't make the world go round. It is the social constructs we put in place that makes the world go round. Whatever we value now or in the future is what makes the world go round. We can change our own behaviors and influence others to create new social constructs and value one thing over another more or less. As soon as we detach ourselves from these social constructs then we could create our reality and focus on creating value for ourselves, for the people around us, and for society as a whole.

dogma #9

"Have it all"

DOGMA #9: HAVE IT ALL

"The way of the Essentialist means living by design, not by default. Instead of making choices reactively, the Essentialist deliberately distinguishes the vital few from the trivial many, eliminates the nonessentials, and then removes obstacles so the essential things have clear, smooth passage. In other words, Essentialism is a disciplined, systematic approach for determining where our highest point of contribution lies, then making execution of those things almost effortless."

– GREG MCKEOWN, ESSENTIALISM: THE DISCIP-
LINED PURSUIT OF LESS

I t is Monday. I have filled my schedule to the brim for the week. My task list is still full of the carryover tasks that I didn't get done from the past week. I have back-to-back meetings from 9 a.m. to 5 p.m. When am I supposed to get work done? Well, I thought I figured out the secret to productivity. I just had to wake up earlier than everyone, at 6 a.m., and get tasks done before all of the meetings. I did this day in and day out. I felt so overwhelmed, exhausted, and... burned out.

I got into technology at an early age. I indulged myself in books and knowledge about building and scaling technology. And I loved it. At 18, I was already interning at a big tech firm working on cutting edge Internet of Things technology. I would quickly rise to the occasion and get rewarded for my ability to distill information, learn very quickly, and my passion for the industry with more and more opportunities. I would be the first pick whenever there is a new major project that comes into our team. I became so obsessed with succeeding, accomplishing more, and building onto my success that I continued to read more, learn more, and pursue everything I could with the same amount of enthusiasm and passion.

I said "yes" to everything. I was so hyperactive and wanted to do everything and anything that comes into my horizon. I quickly lost touch of what was essential and activities that would create strong inflection points in my growth. I was making an inch of progress into a million directions. I became so burned out very quickly.

Burn out — the two words that any sleep-deprived achiever dreads hearing, feeling, and experiencing.

Media platforms and influencers have convinced me that I had to keep striving for more and achieving greater. It was the virtuous cycle of success. Once you achieve something, you have to then go back and achieve the next level of success after that, starting all over again. I thought that I had to have it all - the money, fame, and fortune.

This is the danger in the democratization of mediums at which we can document and share experiences with others. Before the Internet, the only form of storage and accounting was paper, physical mail, and ledgers. Now, we have abundant access to documentaries through vlogs and accounting of other people's experiences. And because we are social animals and we tend to rely on other people's acceptance, we tend to only share the upsides, the accomplishments, and the finished products to others. These then lead the audience to yearn for more — "If they can have it, then I can too."

It is now easier than ever for us to visualize the end of the tunnel and what success could look like. The danger is that we want all of it—every ounce of success and experiences others show on the media.

Despite the breadth of information we now have and documentaries of other people's lives, we need to remember that less is more and that there are only a few things that are important to our goals and our wellbeing.

Always be editing. In this age of abundance, we have to always be cautious about what we are saying "yes" to and the things we are adding. We have to be editing and self-reflecting — focusing on the things that matter to us, our goals, and our well-being.

You don't always have to have it all. You don't have to have all that everyone else has. You get to choose what is important to you and then pursue it fearlessly.

PART 2: DOGMAS OF HEALTH

"Work hard and put in 100 hours a week to be successful."

I bought into all of it. I was hustling and grinding like crazy since I could legally start working in the States (age 16). I would punish myself for wanting to watch Netflix or take a break.

In college, I spent many weekends cooped up in the library. I spent many all-nighters studying and working in the library—pumped with Adderall. My study buddy during those nights had ADHD and would share his supplies with me. I took on everything I could possibly take on in college.

I took every student worker job on campus imaginable, including working as an undergraduate researcher, a note taker, a tutor, and a teaching assistant. I would punish myself for doing anything else or taking a break.

I also had a very minimal and frugal lifestyle. At some point, I was living with my brother and slept on his couch. I would eat microwaveable, quick-and-go meals, and made myself sandwiches to go, which I would eat while studying, working, or commuting.

And I was okay with it. I constantly told myself that this is what I needed to do in order to succeed and do something great with my life. It was what I was getting bombarded with the autobiographies and motivational YouTube videos I was feeding my mind with.

I also only surrounded myself with friends that shared the same grind mode mentality as I did. I cut off friends who only wanted to go to parties or play video games on the weekends.

I always kept myself very busy. I bought into the idea that being busy is what's required to be successful. I was always too busy for everything else. I was too busy to give my body a break. I was too busy to hang out with other people and cherish relationships. I was too busy to take care of my health.

And I got sick. I got sick a lot. The lifestyle took such a toll on my health.

There must be a better way. I realized that I need my body to be functioning at its best to be able to actually do the things I want to do, to be able to create meaningful things, and leave an impactful legacy in the world.

dogma #10

"Trade your health for success"

DOGMA #10: TRADE YOUR HEALTH FOR SUCCESS

"Man! Because he sacrifices his health in order to make money. Then he sacrifices money to recuperate his health. And then he is so anxious about the future that he does not enjoy the present; the result being that he does not live in the present or the future; he lives as if he is never going to die, and then dies having never really lived."

– DALAI LAMA

R eading the biographies of so many of the greats and being bombarded by success stories, I subscribed to the hustle culture.

In college, I sacrificed my health and well-being to achieve success and build a great resume. I had thought that it was just the price you pay to be successful. I bought into the notion that you have to trade your health for success.

For many years, I was a coffee-drinking machine who experienced brain fog and got sick a lot. I would cure and intervene sickness by just "sucking it up" and working even more, because what I thought I had to do.

Working 100-hour workweeks doesn't leave you enough time to think about your health and well-being.

Now imagine a world where many of the greats, like Steve Jobs and Nikola Tesla, are still healthy and alive even when they're 100 years old. I wonder what kinds of innovations and new things in the world they would introduce. I realized that health is really important, especially if you're looking to be successful, change the world and leave a legacy in the world.

I came to the realization that my health is more important than impending deadlines and working long hours. The instant that I prioritized my health and well-being, I started performing very well. I came to work level-headed and with a clear perspective. I remembered things so much clearer. I didn't get burned out so quickly and so often. The momentum was so much more stable.

I could actually see myself doing what I was doing when I was 80 years old. I could see myself working at the same pace and at the same intensity even when I retire.

You do not have to trade your health for success. In fact, your health is a key multiplier for your success. The healthier you become, the clearer you could think and the more hours you could productively and efficiently work, because you have the right kinds of input to output something.

At the same time, we are not machines. You can't expect yourself to just be constantly outputting. Even machines need electricity to power. You need to give yourself a break, because that's part of your inputs.

Health is a multiplier to your productivity. The more hours you work doesn't necessarily mean the better and the higher quality you output. You have to play the long game. Sleeping for the right amount of time, say eight hours a night vs de-priving yourself with three to four hours instead, could mean you can't output post-your 40's. You may already be bed ridden then with how you're overworking yourself in your early 20's. It is just not sustainable.

dogma #11

"Leave it to the professionals"

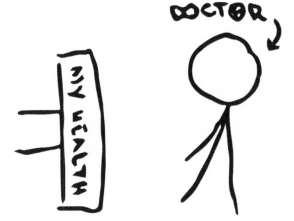

DOGMA #11:
LEAVE IT TO THE
PROFESSIONAL

"Biohacking is really about reclaiming our power. It's saying, "I want to work collaboratively with the physician, but I don't want to turn my power over to them, and say... I'm stressed out. I'm bitch-y. What d'you got for me?" You know... the first option is to take SSRI. We should be going back to, "Okay, what's really going on?" Now, the average doctor's visit lasts about seven minutes."

– DR. SARA GOTTFRIED, MD

I t was a summer in Turin, Italy at a startup accelerator program when I was first exposed to "biohacking." It was 2015 and the term was mainly used by Silicon Valley techies and the occasional Spartan racer. The session was munged among our lecture sessions on finding a product-market fit and getting funded by a venture capital. The session felt out of place, but in the end, it made sense.

Entrepreneurs are problem solvers. They tend to want to do things differently and change the world for the better. And these so-called "biohackers" do exactly that, just on their health and well-being. Now it made sense, why we had biohacking sessions during a startup accelerator program.

I grew up with information in my fingertips. Since I was young, I've always been fond of knowledge and growing my mind in various ways possible. Biohacking is in a way, how us laymen (a.k.a. non-medical professionals) live to extend what's possible and optimize how our bodies function. It is figuring out "What's the best path for *me*?"

It is the way everyday beings are empowered to take control of how their bodies function and react to the world around them. Looking at it in that lens, I think that's so empowering and exciting!

This was such a whirlwind in my head. I've always thought that I had to leave everything up to my doctor or to a professional. For many of us, we only really see our doctor for one to two times a year, so we very rarely check-up how our health is doing and seek interventions.

Now with biohacking, I've felt empowered to really hone in on my health every single day. This new paradigm encouraged me to seek ways to quantify my health and well-being a lot more than one to two times a year. This is not to replace or completely revoke my annual or semi-annual visits to my physician. Instead, it is to work in a more synergistic way with health professionals.

Now I'm able to bring more information about my health and my body and have results from a longitudinal study, because I'm quantifying my health every day compared to the four to five minutes of each year that I can see my doctor and have him assess my health.

This now allows me to work in conjunction with my physician. I know my body way more than my physician could test in a span of a few minutes during an annual exam.

For interventions to be accessible to the masses, they have to be widely tested and examined with a diverse-enough sample with often an intervention and a placebo. This methodology is proven and has allowed us to provide the necessary drug interventions for many decades. However, it isn't without flaws.

First, medical research and tests prior to the 21st century were conducted with mostly male subjects and prior to living in a globalized era, tests were conducted on local subjects that resided close or in the physical area where the test is being conducted. Innately, tests didn't have a diverse enough sample to consider the results significant enough and appropriate for generalization. Every body is different — how your body reacts to certain interventions could be completely different even if the test sample shared a similar genetic makeup as you. Generalized interventions is only the tip of the iceberg, not only do we need to see how each interventions is impacting a certain gender, certain race, or even certain economic standing, but we also have to precisely target and retest interventions for each of our specific, diverse microbiome and the ecosystem that lives within each of our bodies.

Secondly, cutting-edge interventions take a while to get to market and become accessible to the masses. Nowadays, we are able to conduct exams with a diverse sample; however, it also means that interventions are highly regulated and may take years to actually be available in your local pharmacy or even for your physician to be allowed to prescribe it to you. The peril is the profession has a strong divide between the practicing physician and the medical researcher. Take, for example, T. S. Wiley at the American Academy of

Anti-Aging Medicine. Wiley is a researcher instead of being titled a medical doctor, because Wiley's work lies in both her detailed understanding of how hormones work combined with self-experimentation. She is beholden to leaving her work as medical literature, instead of making it the status quo in medical practice, out of fear of losing her license. She self-experiments her own discoveries and has found many effective interventions that she is not allowed to share to patients as a medical doctor.

Now, with information and our own drive to living a healthy, nourished life, we could take in the best of what cutting-edge science produces and precisely target our own genetic makeup and diverse micro-ecosystem in our bodies.

Information and data are widely accessible. We could take control of our own destiny, and really hone in on proactively seeking what could help us be the healthiest we could be. This is also dependent on our daily decisions to actually seek to be the healthiest we could be.

dogma #12

"Life is short"

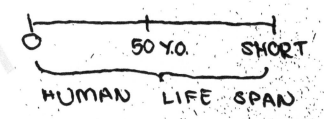

DOGMA #12: LIFE IS SHORT

"Science has begun to demonstrate that aging is a disease. If it is, it can be cured."

– UNKNOWN

Ever since we domesticated fire, we've been augmenting the natural way of life. We've been extending life expectancy and our quality of life. It is one of the things that makes us uniquely human. We've been using our ingenuity to surpass what is naturally feasible.

Amidst learning about this whole world around biohacking, I've also come across the idea that aging is a disease, and it is something we can defeat and cure, just like cancer.

Life doesn't have to be short.

We can intervene and focus on alternatives to lengthen our lifespans and our quality of life by learning from how the "Blue Zones" live. The "Blue Zone" is an area where a significant amount of the population has lived up to or beyond 100 years old. These patterns are found in the way that they eat, socialize, sleep, drink and even the way they approach death.

In Okinawa, a blue zone in Japan, they tend to have a social network of lifelong friends that supports them well into old age.

Even in the our early days, there were naysayers. People who didn't believe in fire. Our ancestors were the ones who adopted fire, because they were the species that continued to live. They found a way to make use of fire to keep their bodies warm in the cold days and cook food, so that we could get more nutrients from it and not suffer from any food-borne illnesses.

Just like the domestication of fire, we could augment our bodies in order to live a longer, fuller life. Longer and fuller—both is important. Just like within our bodies, over time, we develop what's called senescent cells, which are cells that don't die but are in fact already dead in a way that they do not benefit your body any longer. They're like zombie cells. They live a long time, but they no longer benefit your body the same way. We not only need to strive for a longer life but also have to ensure that we are extending the good quality years, as if you're 20 years old living in an 80-year-old body.

We could age backwards with interventions, whether it's feeding your body with the right kind of nutrients it needs or removing toxins from your environment. I've proven this to myself after taking the Gut Intelligence and Health Intelligence test with Viome. It tests for your biological age based on the health of your cells. I've quantified my body 90 days prior, focused on nourishing my body, and re-tested to find out that my biological age is three years younger than my actual age based on the health of my cells.

Life doesn't have to be short, and you can intervene your aging and age backwards—striving to live as if you're in your 20's when you're in your 80's.

Even the genetic makeup and predispositions of your body can be influenced. We are born with genes that we've inherited, and each gene has a predisposition for something negative or positive. What you do to it and the environment you expose to it exaggerates either the negative or positive. There are genes that are predisposed to increase your chances of cancer or diabetes, while those same genes also increase your mental acuity and immunity.

I think it is actually our moral obligations to pursue living a longer, thriving life. We could do more as a society. We could take all of the wisdom we would have gained for living a long lifetime and still be strong and sharp enough to share those experiences, create something of value and contribute to society in more meaningful ways thanks to the amount of years we've lived on this planet.

dogma #13

"Just take the medicine"

DOGMA #13: JUST TAKE MEDICINE

"Let food be thy medicine, and medicine be thy food... Natural forces within us are the true healers of disease."

– HIPPOCRATES

Health professionals focus on medicine, not nutrition or well-being. In most cases, they are trained to prescribe medicine as intervention to sickness and diseases. When you go to your doctor and say that you're depressed or feeling ill, the instinctual intervention is to prescribe you with a Selective Serotonin Reuptake Inhibitor instead of really finding out the reason why you're feeling that way. It could be that you just lost a family member, got laid off, or eating food that doesn't nourish your body.

The average doctor's appointment in the United States lasts for seven minutes. That is not at all enough time to do any kind of root cause analysis. And most often, medicine is not always the right cure.

Medical professionals get paid to prescribe you medicine. Hospitals make money when they charge your insurance company or you for the medicine, they prescribe you. Systematically, doctors are incentivized to prescribe you to just take medicine.

Pair this system with a lot of people not knowing enough about their own health and body leads to so many diseases and illnesses that could have been prevented and more proactively treated.

Medicine is not the cure for everything. We, ourselves, are the only ones who have the ability to test out alternatives and conduct proper root cause analysis with respect to our health. As professionals trained with a scientific mind, doctors rely on treatment and cure based on a sample of people. They do try to prescribe you with treatment based on findings from research on people as similar to you as possible.

The best way of testing what works for you and what doesn't will come from results and studies done on you based on a long period of time. This type of study may not always be economically viable for the entire population, which is why your doctor can't just do this kind of test on you.

Your best bet to finding the best cure for yourself is for you to try and test things out for yourself for a long duration of time. And then, collaborate with your physician on findings of these interventions.

You now reclaim control over your health, as opposed to solely relying on your physician. Now you can work collaboratively and synergistically with your medical professionals to do what's best for you, not what's best to a sample size of people that may or may not be similar to you and your circumstances.

That is not to say that there aren't doctors that practice natural remedies and holistically look at your health. There are, but in many cases, they just don't spend enough time with your body than you to be able to assess what's good for your body at any given period. You are the only person who truly wants the best for you and can know what is best for you at any given time.

Certain interventions and diets may be good for

someone else and may be delivering the results you've been looking for, but that doesn't necessarily mean the effects on you will be the same. Our hormones, our microbiomes, our genetics are different from one another, so we shouldn't expect for the same regimen, the same diet, and the same workouts to work the same way on everyone.

dogma #14

"Focus on what's wrong"

DOGMA #14:
FOCUS ON
WHAT'S WRONG

"Systems thinking is a discipline for seeing wholes. It is a framework for seeing interrelationships rather than things, for seeing 'pattens of change' rather than static 'snapshots'."

— PETER SENGE

A peril of only relying on health professionals to optimize your health is they could only treat you based on what's wrong—commonly asking, "Where does it hurt?" The danger of this is most often, when something is wrong with our health, it is a systematic problem.

This goes back to professionals prescribing those who are depressed and stressed with SSRIs. Being stressed could have been a more general problem caused by the food that they're eating, the frequency at which they're staying active, conditions at work, and more.

We need to treat problems holistically, and we need to optimize our health holistically as well. Your mental health is just as important as your gut health, and your physical strength is just as important as your mobility and flexibility.

Your body is a system, and systems are interconnected and interdependent.

For many months now, I have started the journey of measuring my body. There's a management adage that goes, what doesn't get measured doesn't get managed. I've started to do just that. It is how biohackers operate. The scientists and engineers are the ones that understand the mechanisms behind it all and the reasons why certain things happen in our bodies, while for a biohacker, it is about self-experimenting, trying newly found techniques out, and then measuring. Measuring allows us to quantify exactly how our own unique biology reacts to certain treatments and interventions. Quantifying is the key to this trial-and-error paradigm.

I started quantifying my gut health through

Viome's consumer-facing service. As it goes, you send your stool sample via your local post office and then in return, you get results about your gut, the microbiomes in them, and recommended foods that respond well to your gut ecosystem and those that cause inflammation. Having already learned that your gut health is the root of your overall health, I figured that measuring my gut health would be a good first start.

It didn't only give me the ins and outs of my gut, but it also empowered me to understand what exactly goes in and out of my body and how each food I eat uniquely impacts my body. I did the test at the same time as Jing, my partner-in-life. He had different food recommendations as I did, so we had to alter our routines and meals a bit. I was eating rice while he was eating millet as our carbs. Then, after following the food recommendations for 90 days, you were asked to send another stool sample by mail for a retest. Gladly, most of my scores improved, and the hard work of diligently following what's good for my gut paid off. Then, the same company introduced a new service that would seek out to understand your overall health through a blood sample, which includes your mitochondrial and immune system health. Your mitochondria is the powerhouse of your cells, and you have cells all over your body, while your immune system leads the charge in fighting foreign invading bacteria and viruses in your body.

The results were fascinating and empowering at the same time. For the first time, I understood exactly what happens to my body when I input a certain food. I could self-experiment and see the results right away. I then went out to explore other means of quantifying your body, such as sleep measurements. Then, I understood how interconnected our entire system is.

Changes in my diet and the length of my workouts would not only cause or reduce inflammation, but also lengthened the deep sleep I got that night. Our bodies are like black boxes that take in inputs (e.g., food, sleep, sunlight, stress) and then spits out results (e.g., energy, mental acuity, stress response). I say black box, because I believe there is still much to be learned about our bodies and how it responds to certain stressors or inputs. The democratization of information and accessibility to self-experimentation more than any other point in history are empowering us to unravel that black box and understand more deeply what actually is happening to our bodies.

I believe that in the near future, we would have trained models of our how our bodies work to a point, where we could start with the result or the output in mind (e.g., mental acuity), and then know exactly what we need to tweak and focus on in a more holistic approach.

This is actually not a new concept. In fact, many ancient practices, like ayurveda, focus on a holistic approach to health and wellness. Now, more than ever, we are at a point of history in which more and more people are looking to take back control in their health, information is more accessible and experimentation datasets are widely shared.

Especially in the western world, health and wellbeing have treated reactively. You treat what's wrong, and focus on what's wrong. Instead, we need to be focusing on looking out of your body holistically. Take, for example, 3% of the population suffer from having dandruff. Often, the cure is to recommend some remedy with antibacterial properties that, counterintuitively, actually stop skin cell growth. If we understand the fact that anything that happens to your body externally, whether it's having dandruff, losing hair or dry skin, is caused and is a sign of your internals malfunctioning. Instead of finding an external cure on an external issue, focus on finding out if there are certain deficiencies in your body, if you're not exercising enough, if you're getting stressed, or if the food you're eating is causing inflammation to your body. Your body is an interconnected system.

Stop focusing on what's wrong, and instead holistically assess the situation and remember that your body is an interconnected system.

dogma #15

"When I become successful,
then I'll be happy"

SUCCESS ⟶ HAPPINESS
dependency

DOGMA #15: WHEN I BECOME SUCCESSFUL, THEN I'LL BE HAPPY

"When we are happy—when our mindset and mood are positive—we are smarter, more motivated, and thus more successful. Happiness is the center, and success revolves around it."

— SHAWN ACHOR, THE HAPPINESS ADVANTAGE: THE SEVEN PRINCIPLES OF POSITIVE PSYCHOLOGY THAT FUEL SUCCESS AND PERFORMANCE AT WORK

When I succeed, then I'll do the other things, like travel and nourish friendships. But I've come to realize that happiness doesn't come as an after-thought and that the happier you are now, the more successful you'll become.

I've spent much of my life punting happiness in order to optimize success, or so I thought. I had thought that in order to be successful, you had to sacrifice happiness. After many biographies of the likes of Steve Jobs and Elon Musk, I've come to believe that success comes with many trade-offs and one of those trade-offs is short-term happiness — thinking that when you accomplish something, then you can have success.

If you look up the word "happiness" in the thesaurus, you'll get "fulfillment." Succeeding or accomplishing something is deeply embedded in what it means to be happy. This is in part because traditional psychology research looks at average happiness among so-called "successful people", based on traditional success metrics, like money, fame, and fortune. They have measured happiness as an after-the-fact phenomenon, when in fact, happiness is a daily habit and a lever to success.

There is a certain advantage in success from those who are happy first. In that, the more we feel enjoyment and happiness in the day-to-day imperatives of our careers, the greater we succeed. It's a no-brainer if you put it in that perspective — of course, we are more likely to accomplish more and succeed greater if we love our jobs.

Happiness gives you a performance edge. We perform our best when we feel positive. In my first job out of college, I was promoted after only a year of working there full time. My advantage wasn't necessarily in my experience and wisdom, because I was just right out of college. My advantage was that on average, others were miserable and were performing the jobs as if they were robotic monkeys. I loved the work I did, and when things went south, I saw the positives that we could get out of it. I saw mishaps as an opportunity to be better. "It'll only get better from here," I exclaimed in meetings after I had just confronted a coworker about a mishap. My positive mindset and happiness that I found in the day-to-day fueled my performance and allowed me to produce better work and outcomes.

When others get down about a competitor eclipsing our market capitalization, I feel a boost of energy to do more and take market share back. I saw it as an opportunity as opposed to a setback.

I wasn't born into the best life possible that propelled me to be always happy. I was surrounded by wildly resilient people. When a newscaster filmed a neighborhood that was just flooded by a typhoon, you would always see people smiling to the camera and dancing in the rain.

In the book, "The Happiness Advantage," the author talks about the "Tetris effect," where the effect can be broken down into two variations, first is the negative Tetris effect and second is positive. Psychologists have found that we essentially view circumstances as a game of Tetris, where events fall into place, and we can either view it as positively or negatively shaping our overall outlook. Those who fall into the camp of positively viewing circumstances tend to be more optimistic, set more difficult goals and put in more effort to attain those goals. On the other hand, those that fell into the other camp would have the tendency to only see the weakness and flaws in a situation.

Happiness is a muscle that you have to exercise every day to attain a positive mindset and a positive Tetris effect. By doing so, we increase our chances of succeeding, accomplishing more and feeling great about what we do.

dogma #16

"Aging is inevitable and signs
of aging are normal"

- - - - - - - - -> 100 Y.O.

✓ GRAY HAIR

✓ FORGETFULNESS

✓ IMMOBILITY

✓ SLOW

✓ WRINKLED SKIN

DOGMA #16: AGING IS INEVITABLE; SIGNS OF AGING ARE NORMAL

"I will age with humor, serenity and to the best of my efforts, health. I will continue to express my creativity and personal style. I will challenge the stuck way our culture looks at getting older."

– SOPHIE LUMEN

I magine someone in her 80's, what do you see? Someone whose hair has turned gray, pruny skin, balding, slow to move, no longer has menstrual period and forgets all the time. For too long, we had believed that aging and signs thereof are normal and inevitable. The color of your hair turning gray, your skin wrinkling and your mental clarity deteriorating had been normalized as part of the normal and inevitable cycle of life. We don't have to normalize that any longer.

Humanity has been expanding our life cycles since the very beginning. It is hard-encoded within us to not die. Your body constantly works hard to fight bad actors and strengthen your immune system. It is the fundamental drive of the human race. It is the primary reason why we continued to evolve and adapt. We are just getting started.

Aging is a disease, and we could find ways to cure our bodies from it. Now, more than ever, we have the knowledge and access to extend the average human lifespan. All life forms actually share the same motivations of staying alive, but we are the only species with big enough brains that would allow us to make long-term decisions to support that motivation.

However, the goal is not just to stay alive for a long time, but it is to ensure those lengthened years are lived fully. I am hopeful that we could get there, and that we no longer need to normalize someone in their 80's as someone I described above. Instead, someone in their 80's will be as strong, as beautiful, as flexible and as sharp as they were in their 20's.

Most of us conjure up an image of someone old as someone who's in chronic pain, bound to a wheelchair, and helplessly relying on care of someone else to live. Life can be much more than that. We could lengthen our lifespan and thrive at that. We are the only species who could, so we need to capitalize on that.

Seeing signs of aging shouldn't be normalized at a certain age either. These signs, after all, are merely reflections of how your body is actually doing on the inside. Wrinkles and gray hair shouldn't be treated with external serums or dyes, and instead, we should be focusing our energy on fixing what's inside. These are both signs of our cells dying and no longer rejuvenating as rapidly and as often as they once did. We ought to be looking to tackle that, say by foods that could support our cell growth, quality sleep and exercise.

PART 3: DOGMAS OF WISDOM

There is something so glorious, so freeing and so selfless about writing that we often often overlook. In a way, it is little bits of our mind and memory that get to live outside of our bodies, and if we're lucky, it gets to be passed on to generations to come.

It is a selfless act — we need to celebrate information as fuel for progress.

It is so glorious, that in the age of information, we get to trap these bits of information into a medium that can outlive us. Our human memory is a leaky bucket, and it is such a massive leap in progress that we are now able to jot down information so quickly.

In order for this age of information to take precedence, there needed to be a memory and storage revolution. For when we record and store information, we produce uncorrupted copies of our richly perceived realities.

There is something so interesting with how the world is now taking shape. Everyone is now empowered to document musings and how life goes through social media both in video and in writing.

No longer would the archeologists of tomorrow need to dig up centuries old clay tablets in order to understand the way we lived, the way we interacted and our perceived realities of the world. No longer would lessons learned and key insights be lost only for the next generations to have to re-discover those same insights any longer.

We can now actually just make progress and truly stand in the shoulders of giants.

Information and knowledge intoxicates me. It is the reason why I get so excited with the liberty we have to product and store information.

But there is still no compression framework for wisdom. In that, it is the hours spent day in, day out, of someone learning a craft—experiencing mishaps and shaping the way they do things based on first-hand experience.

I don't claim to have all of the wisdom in the world, nor do I claim to be smarter than anyone who reads this whose age is twice as mine.

I do intend to record and produce memory of what I'm slowly getting a grasp on and how I'm understanding the world.

dogma #17

"Be good at one thing and
stick to it"

DOGMA #17: BE GOOD AT ONE THING AND STICK TO IT

A human being should be able to change a diaper, plan an invasion, butcher a hog, conn a ship, design a building, write a sonnet, balance accounts, build a wall, set a bone, comfort the dying, take orders, give orders, cooperate, act alone, solve equations, analyze a new problem, pitch manure, program a computer, cook a tasty meal, fight efficiently, die gallantly. Specialization is for insects.

- ROBERT HEINLEIN

"How do I find my passion?"

"What do you want to be when you grow up?"

These are the constant nagging voices I had in my mind ever since I was young. When asked what I wanted to do when I grew up, at 7, I wanted to be an inventor; at 8, I wanted to be an astronaut; at 9, a lawyer; at 10, a journalist; at 12, a web developer.

I had so many passions in life and had so many things I wanted to do. Now that I've grown up, the question that I feared the most is, "What do you do?" I feared the question not because I still didn't know what I wanted to do. I feared the question, because I knew I wasn't just one thing and was afraid of being boxed into one thing.

While working as a product manager at a big tech firm, I had other side hustles, including doing marketing and business development consulting, providing graphic design services, running a dropshipping store, and so on, and so on..

Many years later, it seems as if I still haven't found my one-true calling, as many adults lead you to believe.

Many of us get asked the question, "What do you want to do when you grow up?" as early as age 5. If we extend our lives to a 100, that's only 5% of our lives. We've only experienced 5% of what's out there. As a data analyst, that is a statistically insignificant number and correlations made then at that point can be vastly incorrect the more data we collect (i.e., the more time we spend living). Most of the time, our early passions are not the best guide to a lifelong career.

It was the YouTuber, Sorelle Amore, that said, "Passion is not a plan. It's a feeling, and feelings change." If I were to outline my passion, it looks something like this:

At 12, I was immensely passionate about Tumblr and building my own beautiful templates, so I learned HTML and CSS – I'm still intrigued but not as passionate anymore. At 15, I was passionate about fashion blogging and becoming a fashion influencer or designer – got bored eventually. At 16, I was passionate about the cosmos and discoveries about the universe – got bored. At 18, I was passionate about nanotechnology and material science – got bored. At 19, I was passionate about traveling – still passionate about it. At 20, I was passionate about tech, marketing and startups – still passionate about it. I have no idea what the future holds and what I'll be into tomorrow.

It was Steve Jobs that said it so brilliantly, "You can only connect the dots looking backwards." Every little thing that I'm into and what I do on a day-to-day basis can seem insignificant without a single life purpose or a grand plan. Looking backward now, I can totally see how every experience has shaped who I am and what makes me unique.

So get rid of this whole notion that you're only supposed to be good at one thing and you ought to stick to it for the rest of yourself. "Life is not a mystery to be solved but a miracle to be experienced," as Alan Watts says so beautifully.

There are just too many things about the future and about yourself that you don't understand now. You have no idea what the future you is going to be like and is going to like.

In the end, Robert Heinlein once said, "A human being should be able to change a diaper, plan an invasion, butcher a hog, conn a ship, design a building, write a sonnet, balance accounts, build a wall, set a bone, comfort the dying, take orders, give orders, cooperate, act alone, solve equations, analyze a new problem, pitch manure, program a computer, cook a tasty meal, fight efficiently, die gallantly. Specialization is for insects."

What's more, many of the inventions and breakthroughs we now take for granted were byproducts of the combination of vastly different fields and schools of thought. Take, for example, the invention of airplanes by the Wright Brothers and the manufacturing process that was first made efficient by Bill Klann. At the outset, these two significant milestones in humanity may seem like they have nothing in common, but if you look closely, they have a common pattern: the breakthrough was bred out of combining two or more, seemingly different schools of thought and then, in turn, expanding the adjacent possible.

The Wright Brothers were not aeronautical engineers. They were bicycle machinists who were inspired by the idea of allowing humans to venture the skies. When the first plausible airplane took off, the triumph wasn't merely that humans have discovered how to fly, but it was that two amateurs (bicycle makers, no less) had beaten out the best aeronautical engineers in the world.

In the same way, when working at the Ford Motor Company, Bill Klann was a plant manager whose main job was to figure out how to produce two hundred engines per day–an impossible goal at the time. Klann was a jack-of-all-trades and was inspired by his visit in a slaughterhouse where we witnessed millions of hogs, cattle and sheep were being butchered every year. Animal pieces were being cut up piece by piece as they move along overhead trolleys, where each butcher performed a very specific task before sliding the carcass onward. Klann had then figured, if butchers can butcher pigs and cows in that way, they could also build cars in that way. Klann then went on to simplify the process at Ford Motor Company by building a specialized conveyer belt to move parts along a conveyer belt.

At its core, we could fundamentally change the way we do things and create breakthroughs by building upon past ideas and jostling them in a sea of intellect, where we could accumulate insights with profound ways of thinking and a whole new range of combinations. As we connect different things and find new ways of looking at something, we could change the world and expand the adjacent possible.

*One Thing You Can
Do This Week*
The Impossible List

Create an impossible list where you would list down everything and anything you'd like to do and achieve, without any constraints with money, time and ability. What have you been dreaming of doing?

The act of simply creating the list allows you to jot down exactly what you have been dreaming of perhaps in your subconscious mind.

dogma #18

"Follow your passion"

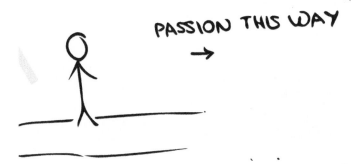

DOGMA #18: FOLLOW YOUR PASSION

"Passion is not a plan. It's a feeling, and feelings change."

- SORELLE AMORE

What I've also come to realize is the adage of "Follow your passion" is terrible advice. To me, it's too much of something I don't have control over—following something that is out there in the ether.

And one of the things that bugs me about it is that if you don't feel that passion, that burning desire in what you're doing now, somehow, you've missed the boat on something that other people knew when they were 18, when selecting their major.

I got so frustrated that I couldn't find my passion and if I did, I would be passionate about something else the next day.

It's as if "passion" is something that's in you intrinsically and you just have to poke around to discover it. The problem with following your passion assumes a constant experience. It assumes that your interests, your worldview, and your environment all remain the same as time passes by.

Instead, what I've found more useful is becoming open minded, widening your aperture to what's possible and filling your life with a bounty of experiences.

The perils are in both words in the phrase—"follow" and "passion". It's as if "passion" is this tangible thing that is somewhere out there, and all you need to do is find it. Secondly, "follow" takes you in this passive, rider role—when in fact, you should be actively driving. And as if what we're passionate about was this whole thing that is constant and not something that gradually develops over time.

The peril is we should not be following our passion, and instead, we should be *developing our pas-*

sions. I actually think this is a better verb. This takes control back to us, as the active driver of our passions, and it encompasses the variable nature of passions.

If I were to just simply follow my passion of writing this book, this book wouldn't have seen the light of day. If I was solely passionate about writing or the contents of this book, I will be dismissive about all of the other things that has to do with building a business around a book, such as marketing, publishing and building a sales funnel.

In the same way, a friend of mine was passionate about graphic design, so he started a design agency. He came at a crossroads in his business, when he suddenly realized that now, he no longer gets to design as much anymore. As the CEO of his new design agency, he now focuses on raising funding, coming up with a business plan, doing sales calls and talking to lawyers.

Today, he is happier than ever, and is still running his design agency. The difference is he has now *developed* new passions and found joy in doing the other things to run his business aside from designing.

◆ ◆ ◆

One Thing You Can

Do This Week
The Three-Year Rule

"I'm just going to try it for three years and see how it plays out."

I needed something that would give my projects a structure. I've been so used to metrics of success, whether it was with grades in school or the ability to move up in a job that I was in. Being my Type-A self, I felt that this whole free-spirited lifestyle of "Oh, I'm just going to do this and see what will happen" was so foreign to me. Having a timeline allowed me to have a structured and disciplined way of creating new opportunities for myself. It gave me the confidence that if it doesn't work out for me, it's not going to ruin my entire life. It became pursuing and creating new opportunities a lot more practical and less scary, and at the same time.

And of course, this three-year rule is arbitrary. For you, this could be six months, one year or five years. More importantly, what you can do is create a form of structure, whether it's a timeline or a financial budget, to new opportunities that you're creating for yourself.

To make something meaningful and successful, it will take some time. In the society we live in today, we've been so spoiled by documentaries of overnight successes. I believe it's because we only notice the greats when they're already great. Oftentimes, we don't see the process and the amount of time for something to pop and become successful. Success takes time, and you have to give new opportunities ample enough time to see the light of day.

dogma #19

"Your degree is your job title"

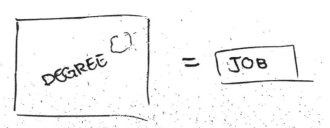

DOGMA #19:
YOUR DEGREE IS
YOUR JOB TITLE

"The important thing in science is not so much to obtain new facts as to discover new ways of thinking about them."

– SIR WILLIAM BRAGG, WINNER OF 1915 NOBEL PRIZE IN PHYSICS

I graduated with two bachelor's degrees—in Applied Physics and in Business Marketing. Throughout college, my double major was both a conversation starter and a confusion. Every single person I meet is intrigued by it. For most, I would get confused looks. How could someone possibly be a Physicist and a Marketer? They just couldn't fathom what my career would be. Yet, I regret nothing about my degree choices in college.

I think that it's a common misconception that your degree has to be what your job title is. What I've come to realize is that the more meta learnings you get from each degree is what's more important.

In Physics, I learned to build a view of the world and have it completely shattered. During the first half of my degree, I learned to build a foundation of how the world works, from the laws of gravity, to mechanics, to thermodynamics. And then, comes junior year, that worldview gets completely shattered and you get introduced to concepts of probabilities, uncertainty principles and a whole-nother view of the world that's even more fundamental than the view that you've just acquired. You also learn to question many things —getting to the bottom of things. A typical tool you use to discover a certain phenomena is to ask "Why" five times until you get to the fundamental reasons why something happens.

"Why is the sky blue?"

"Why do gases and particles in Earth's atmosphere scatter rays of light?"

"Why is it only blue?"

"Why does blue light scatter more?"

"Why does blue light travel as shorter, smaller waves?"

You develop a very prudent way of getting to the bottom of things. You develop a habit of not taking anything at face value and create a view of the world that logically makes sense and can be tested in repeat experiments.

Treading college with a group of peers in a pro-nerd subculture, I know too well that among my peers, there was a strong disdain for "soft" skills and business majors. I very rarely mention to someone who was in or studying the sciences, maths, or engineering that I was also a business major. I was so scared that they will treat me differently and assume that all I want to do is party every night.

In my group of physics study buddies, it was always all about how late you've stayed up all night proving the Photoelectric effect or finding the Fourier series of periodic functions. Learning a fifth programming language was a badge of honor. The number of research papers you've read in a day is a testament to how diligent you were.

When it came time to our senior year, a fraction of us went on to pursue doctoral degrees (a Master's degree in Physics wasn't a thing since it was thought of to be a waste of time and that you'll never get any meaningful research done in just a span of two years), and a fraction of us went to work for companies as software engineers, process engineers or in-house researchers in industry.

Both paths required either a resume or a curriculum vitae (CV). Even then, having a glimmer of "soft" skills were looked down upon. We were told by many of our research advisors and professors to focus on our research findings, the programming languages we know of, and the tools we know how to use.

In a very different world, in Marketing, you learn to assess people's decision-making psychology. You learn about the different dynamics that come into play in making something successful, whether it's in a new territory or industry. You get to understand why certain things appeal to certain people to do something.

With class projects, we almost always worked in teams. In general business classes, during your first and second year, you work in an interdisciplinary group with those majoring in supply chain management, finance, business data analytics, and marketing. As you get to your third and fourth year, you focus on your major's topics, so most of my classes focused on marketing, and group projects were filled with aspiring Marketers.

My confident personality and taste for perfection led me to be the group leader in almost every group project I was on, so I developed strong leadership and communication skills. We worked on many real-world problems and scenarios, even had simulation games to simulate the scenarios you could be put in if you were to introduce a product line in another country or if you were to change your pricing strategies. The simulation models allowed us to develop a strong business sense and learn to be aware of the business landscape from multiple facets, including environmental changes in politics, consumer behavior, and market trends.

I knew I needed both sides. The stark difference in both fields and the attitude of the people in them were scenarios I wanted to keep putting myself in.

I knew I needed to learn both the hard and soft skills from both degrees. I've come to realize that these so-called "soft" skills were not skills that are easy to learn therefore it's not worth putting it in your resume or CV, when in fact, they are the skills that are hard to automate and hard to teach using textbooks.

Physics students who studied the field just five to seven years earlier than I did were taught to use the programming language Fortran, because most experiments, whether it's a particle accelerator or telescopes, were coded in Fortran. Just a few years later, every single research lab started to use Python, so now, all of a sudden, all of your Fortran taxonomy and skills are useless.

Tools and programming languages can rapidly change, even within the span of eight years — that's how long it takes to get a Bachelor's degree and a postdoctoral degree. By the time you've finished school, the "hard" skills you have may very well be outdated.

On the other hand, the meta-learning and the "soft" skills you know will still be relevant. We are social animals, so teamwork, leadership and communication skills will always remain relevant. These are the skills that will be difficult to teach a computer; therefore, they will remain human.

These are the kinds of meta-learning I wanted to learn when I decided what I was going to study in college. I knew that specifics like the 4 P's of marketing or Schrodinger's equation can be forgotten (and easily accessed again through the Internet), but the more meta learnings you get are what can shape the way you view the world and approach problems will remain relevant.

My degree in Physics taught me to be diligent and prudent about building a fundamental view of the world and to become comfortable to have it completely shattered. My degree in Marketing taught me to be retrospective about people's behavior and decision making and to develop a strong business sense and leadership skills.

This is why I believe that your degree doesn't necessarily have to be your job title.

The person you become, the habits you form, and the way you view the world could be completely different from the traditional degree to job title progression.

In my first job out of college, I worked as a product lifecycle engineer/manager for a big tech firm. My days were spent analyzing data, assessing consumer behavior, talking to customers, and developing business strategies that will satisfy customers, shareholders, and the market. In a way, it was the perfect mash of both of the fields I was trained on.

Extracting meta-learnings and "soft" skills are what's needed in the 21st century. This is how we can excel in our careers. Other specific tasks about remembering what the 4 P's are can be outsourced, easily accessed through the Internet, and automated, but all of the meta learnings are hard to codify in a machine or automate.

Instead of thinking of degrees as specific bodies of knowledge, I instead think of degrees as a way of thinking.

dogma #20

"Travel when you retire"

GO
Y.O. → TRAVEL!

DOGMA #20:
TRAVEL WHEN
YOU RETIRE

*"A mind that is stretched by a new experience can
never go back to its old dimensions."*

– OLIVIA WENDELL HOLMES

Since moving to the United States, I've traveled to more than ten countries in the span of four years. No, it isn't because I had wealthy parents that could fund my travels. Traveling is a luxury, and I prioritized it as much as I prioritized going to school. A portion of my paycheck would go to a savings account that's solely dedicated to traveling. I understood how powerful traveling could be.

My family migrated to America in my late teens, which means I've already solidified many of my beliefs in how the world works and a certain way of living. All of that got shattered the moment I stepped into another country.

Not only did I learn a whole new way of living, but for the first time, I also saw my native country from another perspective, as a foreigner. I started to realize the dogmas that shaped who I was and the biases in the way I was living.

For the first time, I saw my native tongue and culture from a different perspective. This perspective allowed me to grow, question things and constantly challenge myself to find better ways of doing things.

Moving to another country is difficult. Partly because you start to become a foreigner on both sides. All of a sudden, I wasn't "Filipino enough" for my friends back home, and I knew I wasn't "American enough" for the States. I started to become bilingual and also started to forget certain words from my native language. I started dreaming and thinking in English, and all of a sudden, I lost touch to my Filipino roots. It became more and more difficult for me to keep a conversation in my household purely in our native tongue because now, I've fully adopted English.

When you first start learning about a language, in conversations, you hear what someone is saying, then translate that to your native language, then process and think of a response in your native language, then translate your response back to the foreign language, and then respond. You collect information in one language but have to digest and process it in another language.

Once you start becoming fluent, you now just instantly collect, digest and process information in that language. Your thought process becomes a lot more instant and streamlined. That's the beauty of practice until the process becomes second nature.

The tricky thing is when you have to think and process information in multiple languages at the same time. This is when you forego certain information from one language.

That's the beauty of traveling, and why I no longer subscribe to the dogma that you get to travel only when you are past retirement age.

I've learned so much in such a short span of time during my time traveling. It is my way of constructing a view of the world. I no longer just blindly accept others' view of the world and how people act. I've come to realize that you learn more accurately and more rapidly how others live in another country by actually going there and internalizing how they do things.

Traveling is so important for us to not only learn about how others on the other side of the world live, but also to have our perspectives in life be completely shattered. This is when we can grow and expand our minds.

It is so important for us to build a view of the world and have it completely shattered. It challenges our minds to continue to expand, dance with new ways of thinking, and continuously assess what could be old dogma that no longer makes sense to follow.

I met a very interesting man at work once who seemed to be very interested in other people's businesses. I don't blame him—people are very interesting once you get to know them and nourish relationships. The first time we met, I opened up to him so freely. It was probably because he empathized and was genuinely curious. One of the things I'd shared with him is that months prior to our conversation, I had taken a solo, backpacking trip to New Zealand for a month. He couldn't fathom why and inquired—trying to conclude if I was just an introverted person or if I just didn't have friends who wanted to travel with me.

I see traveling as a sacred passage into something. In a way, I wanted to get to know the world without worrying about someone I knew judging where I wanted to go or staining my view of the place. I wanted to come to a country with a fresh perspective, open to absorbing everything around me without any preconceived notions and biases.

I've been on overseas trips before with others. The trips always ended up either with disagreements about what day activities we wanted to go do or getting wasted at the beach. But this time, I wanted my New Zealand trip to be different.

I packed a backpack with a week's worth of clothes and plenty of hiking gear. Going in, all I knew about New Zealand was how beautiful and picturesque it was. I booked an incoming ticket to Auckland in the north island and an outgoing ticket from Queenstown in the south island. How I was going to get from point A and point B was something I had to figure out once I got there.

After all, I did not have time at all to plan it out, so the spontaneity was both out of my adventure-seeking personality and convenience. I took the trip the week after my undergraduate graduation. I only had the weekend after the ceremonies to pack and plan my trip, since the months prior to it was fraught with thesis deadlines, job applications and final examinations.

In those four weeks of solo traveling the country, I visited so many towns and cities, met so many new friends, and danced with new ways of thinking. Day after day, I was hiking mountains and terrains throughout the country. I've never had that much time to myself and for self-reflection since then.

Prior to the trip, my mind was always racing from one deadline to the next, bombarded with what I ought to do to become successful and hustle with no sleep. I've never actually reflected about where I've been, where I am and where I want to go, nor did I ever really think for myself about the person who I want to become.

Since that trip, I've put so much value in experiences where I can self-reflect, think and assess the situation for myself without being too caught in the day-to-day business of the world.

dogma #21

"It all goes downhill from here"

DOGMA #21: IT ALL GOES DOWNHILL FROM HERE

Widen your relationship to time, slow it down. Don't see time as an enemy but an ally. It provides you with perspective. Aging doesn't frighten you. Time is your teacher

- ROBERT GREENE, THE LAWS OF HUMAN NATURE

For as long as I could remember, my mom, who's been my role model, has always been this cheerful, always joking around type of woman. No matter how old she gets, she's always been loving life. Her laugh is so loud that you can hear her laugh from two campsites away whenever we would go camping. No matter where she goes, she always carries this sense of wander and admiration for the world.

In my eyes, she has completely shattered every single dogma of what's okay and not okay to do when you get to a certain age. To this day, she's still very active on social media, posting Instagram stories and connecting with so many people.

I think that as we age, whether we're turning 25 or 50, we get told this adage of "It all goes downhill from here." But my mom has proven, time and time again, whether she's turning 30 or 50, that it does *not* go downhill from here, and you can choose not to.

My Instagram-loving, selfie-capturing, world-traveling mom does everything. Not once does she say she's too old for something. She just does it, and it makes her love and enjoy life so much more.

In reality, as we age, it all goes *uphill* from here.

Not only have we experienced and witnessed more about the world, but have we also matured our thinking. There isn't a compression system for wisdom. You need practice and aging to mature your thinking.

The fact that my mom still chooses to experience and enjoy the world as if she's 22 is phenomenal. No one can tell her otherwise.

Life is here to be lived. You don't become outdated when you turn a certain age—you become more wise.

In the same way as our ancestors had gathered around the campfire and passed stories and learnings to younger generations, we ought to preserve human experiences and turn them into undying legacies. I think this is what's so appealing about living a longer, fuller life.

It's time to rid of the idea of an old person as someone who's pruny and forgets all the time. The better alternative is if we could live a longer, high quality life, where our minds are still as sharp, our energies are still as full, and our abilities are still as unstoppable as if we were in our 20's. Once we do, we could have 100 year olds telling us of their stories and learnings from the great deal of life they had live, just as with as much passion, energy and sharpness as if they're three-quarters their age.

Perhaps, the reason why scientific breakthroughs are difficult to come by is that as a scientist, you spend much of your time learning about other people's discoveries and building on them as much as you do testing and experimenting your own hypotheses. But what if we could have 100-year-old scientists who have 70+ years of findings over the years? Imagine how much more, we as humans, could achieve and uncover.

In the same way, imagine 100-year-old business executives who could use their 70+ years of experience in various economic and political environments over the years. Nowadays, if you are a businessperson turning 50, it's much harder for you to get up the ranks and earn an executive position if you hadn't done so already. Some would argue it's because the company is trying to save its fortunes on not having to pay for your social security or retirement. That's just such a missed opportunity of being able to capitalize on so many years of wisdom.

We should be changing this narrative. It does not go downhill from here. Get rid of your idea of being old as someone who's pruny and forgetful. Life can be so much greater than that. Let us give some justice to our unique human experiences and honor life and the accumulation thereof as much as we honor youth.

◆ ◆ ◆

One Thing You Can Do This Week
Write Everything Down

There is something so glorious, so freeing and so

selfless about writing that we often often overlook. In a way, it is little bits of our mind and memory that get to live outside of our bodies, and if we're lucky, it gets to be passed on to generations to come.

It is a selfless act — we need to celebrate information as fuel for progress.

It is so glorious, that in the age of information, we get to trap these bits of information into a medium that can outlive us. Our human memory is a leaky bucket, and it is such a massive leap in progress that we are now able to jot down information so quickly.

In order for this age of information to take precedence, there needed to be a memory and storage revolution. For when we record and store information, we produce uncorrupted copies of our richly perceived realities.

dogma #22

"Being educated means having
a college degree"

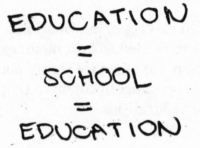

DOGMA #22: BEING EDUCATED MEANS HAVING A COLLEGE DEGREE

"An educated man is not, necessarily, one who has an abundance of general or specialized knowledge. An educated man is one who has so developed the faculties of his mind that he may acquire anything he wants, or its equivalent, without violating the rights of others."

— NAPOLEAN HILL, THINK AND GROW RICH

When I came to the United States, I had to take an English as a Second Language (ESL) class, primarily because I didn't attend an English-speaking high school having come from the Philippines. I remember being taught how to read very clearly like it was yesterday because after all, I took the class at a ripe age of 15.

When we were young, we were taught to read slowly and aloud. When you're learning a new language, you're encouraged to read words out loud. This method helped with our comprehension. For most of us, that's the only phase in our lives when we are ever taught how to read.

Reading is, in fact, a crucial skill that we need to re-learn as we grow older. As we grow older, reading aloud is no longer the appropriate way to deepen our comprehension and learn to read.

Now in the new age, the most crucial skill we could ever learn is to be able to rapidly learn and adapt. To do so, we need to re-master learning how to learn.

As we get older, the same comprehension techniques we are taught while we are young no longer applies. We need to re-look at things with another lens, knowing that now we have greater wisdom about how the world works.

We are taught to learn by regurgitating information in exams, and constantly asking for information learned with the phrase, "Will this be in the exam?" The education system today values regurgitation as opposed to real learning. You don't learn through mistakes or by following your curiosity. Instead, you learn by embodying the predetermined curriculum set forth in your syllabus.

It is an educated condition.

It hasn't yet come to us that we need to re-look at this with an adult's mind once we get older.

With an adult's mind, our comprehension is deepened and we can make connections based on firsthand experiences and impending real-world consequences.

Even after university, we need to own our learning. What we know and what we can do are things no one can ever take away from you. Sure, you could get laid off or have some misfortune happen to your business, but you could still take the skills and experiences you earned to go start something new. You are solely responsible for that.

Knowledge is not power, but instead, it is potential power. It potentially could make you powerful only if you make something out of it. The organization thereof and the actions that you take from the accumulation of that knowledge are what will make you powerful.

It is a learned dogma that we believe that you have to go to school to be educated. There are many powerful people that dropped out or didn't go to school, but they are still educated. Our systems of education only go as far as teaching you what knowledge to acquire and where to acquire it, but it is up to you to organize that knowledge and put it to practical, actionable next steps that could create value to society and make you powerful.

The meaning of being educated shouldn't be based on how many years of schooling someone has taken, but instead, it should be based on someone's ability to acquire knowledge, organize it and then use it. The use and organization of knowledge are what convert your acquired knowledge into actual power from potential power.

Education neither starts nor stops with school. You don't have to start going to school in order to be educated. In the same way, your education does not end when you graduate from school.

dogma #23

"Stay busy to stay productive"

DOGMA #23:
STAY BUSY TO
BE PRODUCTIVE

"What if we stopped celebrating being busy as a measurement of importance? What if instead we celebrated how much time we had spent listening, pondering, meditating, and enjoying time with the most important people in our lives?"

– GREG MCKEOWN, ESSENTIALISM: THE DISCIP-
LINED PURSUIT OF LESS

"Call the front desk office to your apartment," my mom told me for the millionth time. For some reason, I've put off errands for as long as they could last.

I've had packages that I was supposed to return sitting in my room for several months. I've put off gaining money back, because I never called the front desk or the help line.

Until after a year of living in California, I didn't go to the DMV to get a driver's license or a state ID.

I didn't know what it was about.

None of these tasks were that hard. It was "errand paralysis," and being busy for the other things.

It wasn't like I was lazy.

In fact, I got a lot of stuff done—at work. I am on top of everything for all matters that have a direct impact on my career.

I kept myself busy, every single waking hour. It's how we're conditioned. It's in our background music, and the social media influencers we follow.

The culture of hustling, working 100-hour workweeks, and grinding past dawn have been instilled in me since the age I was legally allowed to work a job.

By then, I have bombarded my mind with "Work hard, hustle" mantras from self-help books, Instagram quotes and YouTube motivational videos.

"Do you want to achieve something great? Are you looking to improve your life?"

Consuming self-help content literally gives a surge of dopamine to our brains. The more we consume, follow and read, the more we yearn for more and more and more. It's a no brainer why the self-help development industry is worth billions, and that we are left with media influencers making bank the more self-help content they produce.

Don't get me wrong. This industry has helped and shaped the way I think about things. To it, I owe my knowledge about financial freedom, location-independence and more.

But there comes a time when you realize self-help development content is exactly that—*self* help. You actually have to put in the work and push yourself to do the work. We are drowned with content after content that all we do is consume and consume, because it gives us the rush, the dopamine hit we look for.

We get into self-help paralysis.

I was stuck in this rabbit hole for many months after college. I had just moved to San Francisco in the hopes of making a name for myself and to follow a job in tech. Before then, I had a very busy schedule. I was pursuing two degrees concurrently, had a full-time job, and worked in a research lab. The moment I stepped foot to the "real-world," all of the extra-curricular, multiple jobs at a time, and grades as success metrics were gone.

I felt so empty, and that all of a sudden, I had so much time in my hands. No longer did I have to come home from work just to bury myself in more work for school. I came home to make dinner, wind down and go to bed—and then, do it all over again the next day. At nights, I would consume self-help content in the form of YouTube videos and books as a form of winding down and keeping myself sane, because before then, all I was was "busy." Busy was my go-to state of mind and my excuse to not do anything else but work.

The more I consumed self-help content, the more I wanted to learn more, dive deeper. The YouTube and Instagram algorithms perpetuated my obsession as the platforms would feed me more and more like content to get hooked.

It became an addiction.

Being my perfectionist self, I was paralyzed to actually do work and take on new projects, because I felt like there was still one more piece of content that I was to learn before starting. I was so paralyzed and had no idea why. I knew I was trapped and the only way out is to stop consuming content and start doing.

And since then, I had promised myself not to consume more content if I didn't put the same amount of time into creating. If I were to buy another Kindle book, I had to do something with my newly learned knowledge from the past Kindle book I had just finished reading. I now catch myself, knowing in the back of my mind that self-help content is addicting and the more I consume the more rush I feel from the consumption. I time how much time I spend consuming and allocate that same ratio into creating. The rush I now feel from publishing something or getting positive feedback from something I created is a lot greater than the dopamine hit I get when consuming content. I just had to keep remembering that feeling.

dogma #24

"Never quit"

DOGMA #24:
NEVER QUIT

"For all of the most important things, the timing always sucks. Waiting for a good time to quit your job? The stars will never align and the traffic lights of life will never all be green at the same time. The universe doesn't conspire against you, but it doesn't go out of its way to line up the pins either. Conditions are never perfect. "Someday" is a disease that will take your dreams to the grave with you. Pro and con lists are just as bad. If it's important to you and you want to do it "eventually," just do it and correct course along the way."

— TIMOTHY FERRISS, THE 4-HOUR WORKWEEK

Passion is a feeling, and feelings change.

Luck is a product of the opportunity and the area of opportunities available to you at any given time.

I've never been one to open up to anyone about unfinished projects and talk about new ventures and ideas that I'm still developing in my head. I've had this notion in my head that I can never show the behind-the-scenes of an unfinished project to anyone, because of my fears of failure and never amounting to expectations. I thought that others would think I don't know what I'm doing and that I'm still figuring things out jumping from project to project. And I am, but it was just such a taboo thing to do.

I once believed that some are lucky and get a break or pop early in their careers. They are the 13-year-old YouTube influencers earning six-figure months and the child prodigies who seem to hit gold at an early age. For the rest of us, we are fed into a system where you choose who you want to be and the career you want to pursue at age 18. If you believe me in thinking that we are the generation that will be centenarians, then at age 18, that's only 18% of your life! As a trained scientist, I know that is not a significant sample to make conclusions out of. If we are to be expected to stick to what where we found joy and an industry we felt passionate about from the age of 18 to 60, I think that's a recipe for disaster.

We are of migrant descent.

We've been nomadic species for survival. Following Maslow's hierarchy of needs, we migrated for food and shelter, whether it's running from drought or danger. Then, we started migrating for fortune and opportunities. This is why my family migrated from a third world country to the United States. It was the land of opportunities. And now more than ever, many of us are migrating for self-fulfillment—just look at digital nomads working in Bali, Indonesia.

As it is now less taboo not to be tethered to a specific location and become location-independent, career-jumping also shouldn't be so frowned upon.

I used to believe that some people are just lucky and that they have just found their zone of genius much earlier on.

And I'm here to tell you that they are just lucky, but I don't mean chance. You get lucky as you expand the area to where you can pop and hit an inflection point. You get there by widening your horizon and putting your eggs into multiple baskets. You have to expand the arena at which you play to win.

The cemetery is where a lot of regrets and dreams lie, and they're caused by one catastrophic disease: *failure paralysis*. It is when we are paralyzed and tethered to a job, a career, or an industry, because of our fear of failure.

What's more, we live in a culture where we are slammed with "Never quit" and "Just keep going" slogans. Even when that very action degrades our will to do the very thing we used to find a lot of joy in.

We tend to equate productivity with always working. I used to always be busy and never dedicated time to reflect and assess the situation. We forget that productivity is an equation, and that is the product of the effort we input into something and the amount of fun and passion that we feel about that something. This means that we increase productivity by increasing the "fun" factor.

When we tether ourselves to a job that we no longer find joy in, productivity degrades fast.

There is a stark difference between quitting something prematurely before something causes an inflection point that could leapfrog you to exponential success versus working day-in, day-out on a soul-sucking job.

The mind is a curious object, and sometimes you just have to open your closet of curiosities. Stop following the advice of "Never Quit," and instead properly assess when to quit and move on to something better.

One Thing You Can Do This Week
Don't Quit on the Bad Days

Quit when it's truly the right moment to do so,

and you've calculated the risks. You are taking informed risks. Do not quit on the bad days. Let the emotions sizzle out, and assess if when it's a good day, you still want to quit.

dogma #25

"Listen to experts"

DOGMA #25: LISTEN TO EXPERTS

"Opinions are the cheapest commodities on earth. Everyone has a flock of opinions ready to be wished upon anyone who will accept them. If you are influenced by "opinions" when you reach DECISIONS, you will not succeed in any undertaking."

– NAPOLEON HILL

We live in interesting times. We live in a world where novices are quickly becoming gurus. This world is drought ridden with double-edged swords. On the one hand, with marketplaces and platforms, like Skill-Share and YouTube, we are now getting unique perspectives from novices learning a new skill and teaching with a novice's perspective. We get tutorials from someone who still has fresh battle wounds from the agonizing pain of learning something new. On the other hand, we build a self-perpetuating industry of self-help, fake gurus that now spend most of their time teaching versus doing the thing they are teaching.

The self-help, development industry is a billion-dollar industry, so it's a no-brainer that it's an attractive industry.

I'm not saying don't listen to experts at all. What I'm suggesting is to take advice with a grain of salt. This is the knowledge era, and after all, there is no compression framework for experience.

I don't have many mentors, but I have treated books as my mentors. I've learned many insights and much of the wisdom I have from reading books and consuming content online. This has expanded my view of the world and the way I consume information.

We are in a fake news epidemic. The problem is deeply rooted in how we are taught to think. Our school system has been focused on cramming as much information as they can into our brains. This sort of education system made sense in the past when the information wasn't as democratized as how it is now and information was largely censored.

In this era of information, our problem is no longer the amount of information we can access, but it is now the abundance of misinformation and the increasing inability to think for ourselves and critically. As counterintuitive as it may sound, the truth is now, more than ever, harder to find.

To counteract this abundance of misinformation, we have to constantly train our minds to think critically about a certain subject and how to process the amount of information overload we get every day. We ought to take a moment and make it a habit to self-reflect — learn to process relevant information versus irrelevant, or downright fake.

At the same time, listening to beginners could actually give you a lot more value and explain things in a way that resonates to you, if you're a beginner in that field, too. Most likely, experts are fraught with jargon and just plainly, a different way of seeing the world through certain frames of mind of which they're an expert in. A beginner could teach another beginner differently by explaining with fewer jargons and taking you through a first-hand experience of how they learned. An expert may have already forgotten what it was like to be a beginner again and may have forgotten some of the things that they struggled with in the beginning. For a beginner, the feeling of being a beginner and the specific topics that they found hard to understand are still very fresh in their minds, so they could relate that back to you and could explain concepts in simpler terms.

The way I see it, there are three types of teachers in today's age: the true expert, the guru, and the beginner. You have to be cognizant of the differences and understand possible biases that may be coming from them.

The true expert has been in the industry for a while now, and they know the tips and tricks. They could do anything in this industry robotically, without even exerting much brain power. The biases they hold may be not being able to explain what they do clearly, because everything now just comes so naturally to them.

The guru may have been out of the industry for a while, and is now just in the business of teaching. They can tell you what's worked and what didn't in the industry during their time. The bias they hold may be not knowing the state of the industry now, and thus, teaching you old advice that may already be outdated.

Thirdly, the beginners are just getting up to speed with the industry. They are teaching beginners like them, so they could explain concepts in a way that beginners could understand. The bias they hold may be being too naive and not knowing certain advanced topics.

AFTERWORD

This book is not at all about new dogmas to learn, but it is about unlearning dogmas—ideas that we have been bound by, caused by imaginary boundaries. We are fraught with "should be's" and "shouldn't be's". This book is about a different way of thinking, about seeing around corners and questioning beliefs and ideologies.

The world is full of figments of anthropogenic imagination —ideologies, businesses, money, the healthcare system, the stock market, all came from somebody's mind. We don't have to condone it all, and we don't have to make it all the reality we live in.

As we grow up, we tend to get told that the world is the way it is and that your role is just to live your life inside this world. However, that's a very limited life, and it can be much more expansive.

Most of these systems and ideologies were

made by people in certain circumstances and in certain points in time. Certain learned behaviors may already be outdated and may not apply to the life you're living now, at this time and with your own circumstances.

We can create our own realities. We can influence the world, and build our own things that other people could find valuable.

Create your own reality!

Zoë Cayetano

ABOUT THE AUTHOR

Zoë Cayetano

Zoë Cayetano grew up in a small town in Zambales, Philippines, where she spent her childhood years exploring different passions when she wasn't basking under the sun by the beach. She has then moved to the United States and is now based  in San Francisco, California. She's been a competitive sudoku player, photo-journalist, fashion blogger, web developer, systems engineer, particle accelerator research assistant, tech founder, product manager, and online content creator. Zoë was formally trained in the fields of Applied Physics and Business Marketing, where she had pursued her love for understanding the world and then creating something of value for society.

Zoë's eccentric background and many passions in life conjure up a unique perspective in all matters of life. She had been passionate about becoming financially free, hacking biology, and continuously expanding her mind.

In this book, Zoë explores the many dogmas and self-limiting beliefs on Wealth, Health and Wisdom imposed upon us since we were young. Unlearn Dogma is Zoë's first book.

PRAISE FOR AUTHOR

Great work Zoe! The "Be Good at One Thing, and Stick To It" really resonates with me, I've always struggled with feeling like I should be specializing and diving deep on subjects but find myself easily bored and always wanting to find something new to do.

- BRYCE

I just read the free preview of your book, thank you so much for sharing! I agree with everything that's written on it. I love how you pointed out on "be good at one thing and stick to it" section, that there's a lot more to discover about ourselves and neither you nor anyone else is just one thing. I'm a med tech student, I just started writing articles for an online magazine (waiting for them to email me back, since it's my first time), I'm also passionate about business. So that's 3 different things I'm passionate about in life still in progress but yeah, I'm pretty sure that your book is going to be awesome and I can't wait to read the rest of it

- RAINNA

I just read the mini book and cannot wait to read all of it!!!! Love, love, love what I read so far!

- ARSENIJA

It sounds like excellent content that could be especially helpful to junior and senior high school students, guidance and career counselors at high school and college levels and church youth group counselors. It would be a good read for most ages to help in reframing a less risky approach to earning income.

- PATTY

The topic is so fascinating - it has linkedIn written all over it!

- AGGIGIE

Can't wait to do some serious UN learning!

- SOREN

Very inspiring and thought provoking book

- PAUL

first, WOW! every word used in this book resonates with me. It's real, it's amazing and I agree on every aspect. Unlearning dogma is challenging but I'm up for it!

- CLINETTE

YOUR DOGMA
UNLEARNING
IN ACTION

This book is intended to create a new generation of critical thinkers that could shape a world where we no longer blindly conform to dogmas. Dogmas shape our values, which in turn, shape our actions and thoughts.

You should not be doing this alone. You are now part of a family of dogma unlearners. Start with my website, unlearndogma.com. Here, I have aggregated resources, tools and additional information to support your un-learning. You can also sign up to my free e-mail newsletter.

Join the mailing list to stay in touch, and be the first to access new content, resources and courses to support you in your journey to unlearning dogma.

https://www.unlearndogma.com/

Get exclusive access to BONUSES of this book, including worksheets, tool and additional resources.

http://unlearndogma.com/bonuses

I'd love to connect with you online and continue the discussion on dogma un-learning:

Instagram: @zoecayetano

LinkedIn: Zoe Cayetano

YouTube: Zoe Cayetano

Share the book and invite others you know who would benefit from it. Once you get the book, take a photo or video and share it on your social media platforms. Tag me **@zoecayetano** on Instagram. I'd love to see your unlearning in action and see what you end up doing after reading the book!

I look forward to hearing more about your un-learning in action and how you have made this practice your own!

I'd love to hear your thoughts. If you enjoyed the book, please consider leaving a review and sharing your rating on Amazon.

UNLEARNDOGMA.COM

ACCESS BONUSES & RESOURCES / JOIN THE EMAIL LIST

Made in the USA
Las Vegas, NV
20 December 2021

39064260R00114